The Six Laws of Wealth

THE SIX LAWS OF WEALTH

By: D.K. Hawkins
Version 1.1 ~January 2023
Published by D.K. Hawkins at KDP
Copyright ©2023 by D.K. Hawkins. All rights reserved.

No part of this publication may be reproduced, distributed, or transmitted in any form or by any means including photocopying, recording, or other electronic or mechanical methods or by any information storage or retrieval system without the prior written permission of the publishers, except in the case of very brief quotations embodied in critical reviews and certain other noncommercial uses permitted by copyright law.

All rights reserved, including the right of reproduction in whole or in part in any form.

All information in this book has been carefully researched and checked for factual accuracy. However, the author and publisher make no warranty, express or implied, that the information contained herein is appropriate for every individual, situation, or purpose and assume no responsibility for errors or omissions.

The reader assumes the risk and full responsibility for all actions. The author will not be held responsible for any loss or damage, whether consequential, incidental, special or otherwise, that may result from the information presented in this book.

All images are free for use or purchased from stock photo sites or royalty-free for commercial use. I have relied on my own observations as well as many different sources for this book, and I have done my best to check facts and give credit where it is due. In the event that any material is used without proper permission, please contact me so that the oversight can be corrected.

The information provided in this book is for informational purposes only and is not intended to be a source of advice or credit analysis with respect to the material presented. The information and/or documents contained in this book do not constitute legal or financial advice and should never be used without first consulting with a financial professional to determine what may be best for your individual needs.

The publisher and the author do not make any guarantee or other promise as to any results that may be obtained from using the content of this book. You should never make any investment decision without first consulting with your own financial advisor and conducting your own research and due diligence. To the maximum extent permitted by law, the publisher and the author disclaim any and all liability in the event any information, commentary, analysis, opinions, advice, and/or recommendations contained in this book prove to be inaccurate, incomplete, or unreliable or result in any investment or other losses.

Content contained or made available through this book is not intended to and does not constitute legal advice or investment advice, and no attorney-client relationship is formed. The publisher and the author are providing this book and its contents on an "as is" basis. Your use of the information in this book is at your own risk.

TABLE OF CONTENTS.

- TABLE OF CONTENTS. 3
- INTRODUCTION 5
- PART 1 – SAVING 9
  - WHY IS SAVING MONEY SO HARD? HOW AM I TO DO IT BETTER? 10
  - THE FINEST MONEY-SAVING IDEAS OF ALL TIME. 20
- PART 2 – INVEST. 37
  - WHAT IS AN INVESTMENT? 37
  - WHAT ARE THE MANY DIFFERENT FORMS OF INVESTING? .44
  - HOW TO BECOME WEALTHY AS AN INVESTOR. 49
  - HOW TO START INVESTING TODAY WITH THE MONEY YOU CURRENTLY SPEND. 54
- PART 3 - DEBT FREE 61
  - HOW TO UNDERSTAND THE PSYCHOLOGY OF DEBT AND GET OUT OF DEBT. 70
  - BAD DEBT CAN RUIN YOUR WEALTH. 78
  - YOUR STRATEGY FOR REDUCING DEBT. 81
  - CONVERTING DEBT TO WEALTH. 84
- PART 4 – PATIENCE. 89
  - WHAT DOES IT COST YOU TO DEVELOP PATIENCE? 89
  - HOW TO GO FROM BEING DESTITUTE TO BEING RICH. 92
  - MONEY HAS AN ENERGY FIELD. 93

BRINGING YOUR IDEAS INTO BEING....................................96

WHY PATIENCE IS THE CRITICAL SUCCESS ELEMENT..........100

THE FORMULA FOR WEALTH THAT CAN NEVER FAIL..........106

PART 5 - INVEST IN SELF..115

EXCELLENT METHODS TO INVEST IN YOURSELF.................120

PART 6 – DIVERSIFIED. 130

WHY IS DIVERSIFICATION IMPORTANT FOR YOUR PORTFOLIO? 137

THE SIGNIFICANCE OF DIVERSIFICATION FOR WEALTH CREATION. 145

ARE YOU DIVERSIFYING YOUR INVESTMENTS SUFFICIENTLY? 151

INVESTMENT PRUDENCE THROUGH PORTFOLIO DIVERSIFICATION. 163

EXIT TECHNIQUES AND DIVERSIFICATION.........................172

DIVERSIFICATION IS THE KEY TO INDIVIDUAL WEALTH. 178

CONCLUSION. 189

INTRODUCTION.

Among the most important laws controlling the universe are the laws of wealth. These principles relate to the ebb and flow of wealth in our life, and contrary to popular assumption, this law is not that frugal after all.

Do you want to learn more about these laws? Continue reading to learn more about the laws of wealth.

The universe is abundant. Unfortunately, not many people appear to comprehend this, so they attempt to cling to what they have. They do not grasp that prosperity can flow freely; it is not limited. When you relinquish riches, you always receive them back in some form.

Felix Dennis, one of the wealthiest persons in the world, stated that after you have gifted, lent, or donated your money, you should forget about it. According to the laws of wealth, like attracts like. If you align with your request, it will come to you.

Therefore, to attract riches, you must have a mindset that vibrates at the same frequency as your desire.

If you request more money and prosperity while thinking about your bills and financial issues, you will simply attract more bills and financial problems. Before doing anything else, you must cleanse your mind and accept your thoughts and emotions. Ensure that your level of enthusiasm is commensurate with the request you are making.

If you are serious about attracting more wealth into your life, you must quit degrading yourself. The laws of wealth state that negative thoughts create obstacles. You must start shedding these negative behaviors and establishing new, empowering ones. Always keep a smile, especially when performing mundane tasks like washing dishes.

A positive attitude is one technique to filter out negative ideas and start attracting prosperity into your life. As previously said, the laws of wealth are not as frugal as some people make them out to be. The true miser is the individual who holds himself or herself back. It is time to stop thinking this way and start attracting greater wealth and prosperity.

Everything must be explained by a law operating in the background. The absence of legal knowledge does not negate the existence of law. Therefore, a law must explain why John is wealthy and Jim is not, given that they possess comparable skills, backgrounds, and work ethics.

Those who comprehend this law do not find it mysterious. It is not chance or luck. Any scientific explanation eliminates chance or luck. We invoke explanations of luck or chance only in the face of ignorance and uncertainty.

While I or anybody else may not have discovered this law at this time, we may be certain that there is a law of wealth or attraction that attracts money to those who have consciously or unconsciously exploited it.

Every phenomenon and event in the universe can be scientifically explained. A causal connection explains an effect like a person becoming affluent. In the area of human affairs, whereas such a link can be established with absolute certainty through controlled trials, it is more difficult to identify it with complete confidence.

However, individuals with extensive experience in this field assert that you can attract riches by cultivating particular attributes. These characteristics transcend the characteristics of a virtuous person.

Do you want to bring a never-ending stream of money and wealth into your life? Learn the secrets of wealth with the six laws and principles of wealth discussed in this BOOK. If you wish to get wealthy with minimal effort and struggle, then this is your go-to resource.

Read on to learn more.

PART 1 – SAVING.

Did you know how well you manage your finances can be an important indicator of your likelihood of achieving other personal goals? Indeed, the same fundamental principles used to save money or accumulate wealth can also be applied to achieving non-monetary goals.

The process of accumulating wealth might be quite slow. For instance, saving money typically requires us to start with a specific quantity ranging from zero to an unspecified amount. Then, we must design a plan and exercise the necessary self-discipline to implement that plan. Therefore, you must be willing to take little, planned measures to reach your goal.

Shouldn't we follow the same procedure while attempting to achieve other goals, such as improving health or finding a new job?

People just do not seem to get it, yet we accomplish whatever we desire by making modest, incremental efforts. We develop greatness by achieving our seemingly inconsequential, small ambitions.

I urge all my clients and subscribers to develop the habit of saving money often and not saving money to spend but to achieve financial independence and security.

The true beauty of saving money is that, after a certain length of time, it becomes a habit, at which point you will question why you never saved consistently in the past and will want to save more and more.

WHY IS SAVING MONEY SO HARD? HOW AM I TO DO IT BETTER?

So perhaps you recall, as a child, a representative from your local bank visiting your school and speaking to your class about money and saving.

What, then, is a saving? Saving is the act of storing something for future use.

What, then, are money savings? Savings is the amount of money you retain from your income.

Consequently, what is a savings account? A savings account is simply a bank account where savings are kept. The bank will pay you interest (a specified percentage) on the balance in your account.

Why is the bank acting this way?

When you deposit funds at a bank, they can use those funds to lend to others and invest to earn a profit. The bank will pay you a percentage of its earnings in exchange for your permission—a percentage known as the Interest Rate determines this.

But how many of us today have a respectable record of savings?

Back then, we only had to pay for candy and toys. Saving all we ever acquired was simple, but now, it seems much more difficult. You have rent or mortgage payments, auto payments, gas, public transportation, cell phone, landline, internet, electricity, gas, and food, and we have not even accounted for spending money or taxes.

Okay, so after you pay for all these items, you can have enough money left over to deposit into your savings account. This is true for most people. However, remember that everyone has these costs. You can believe that the issue is that you did not receive enough money to start with.

Yes, that can have a role, but it is not the primary issue. How many people in your office, family, or social circle earn high wages but always appear desperate for their next paycheck? This is because, probably like you, they are also making little progress. The bank accounts are almost identical from year to year.

So, what is it if the issue is not how much you receive, and everyone needs to buy the same goods?

Why is saving so difficult?

Let us start by analyzing the ordinary person's funds flow in a savings situation.

- Income comes in Expenses go out
- Whatever remains is applied to [credit card] debt repayment.
- Anything remaining is saved in your bank account.

This seems plausible. However, this approach will never propel you forward. There is nothing wrong with what is being done, but here is the secret: it is all about the order in which they are performed. Let us examine it in the CORRECT sequence.

Income is received. A predetermined quantity of money is deposited into a savings account. A predetermined amount is used to pay down bad debt

Expenses go out.

"What is it?" you remark, "Paying oneself first? You must be kidding me. I cannot pay myself first. I won't have sufficient funds to cover my expenses." And what do you know? You are likely correct.

The first time you examine this in the new arrangement, you will discover that you lack sufficient funds to cover your expenses. However, are you not the one working so many hours? You are the one who got the promotion, right?

Aren't you the one that wants to accomplish all those goals? It is. Therefore, my question is, "Why wouldn't you pay yourself first in the world?"

Do you believe Woolworths or Coles is more deserving of your patronage?

Do you believe the bank is more deserving of your money?

Do you believe the utility company should be compensated more than you do? No. They are not.

This is possibly one of the greatest obstacles you will ever need to overcome to attain the money you desire, but once you do, EVERYTHING becomes much clearer and simpler.

Therefore, how much is the predetermined sum?

If necessary, use your after-tax income. Most sites recommend starting with 10% of your gross income. If 10% is manageable, increase the need to 15% or 20%. If you cannot manage 10%, settle with 8% or 5% instead.

You can believe that 10% is impossible to achieve but let us examine some numbers. If you made $10 daily, could you survive on $9? How easy is it to find $1 if you need it in the future?

What can $10 purchase? You can do lunch at McDonald's one day and a couple of beers at the bar one evening without the $10.

What if you got $1000?

Wouldn't $900 be sufficient to get by without too much drama?

Rest, and you will not miss that 10% if you take it out immediately before considering spending it. The average annual wage in Australia is approximately $42,000 if you could only save 10% of your monthly salary.

You would have $4,200 in your bank account, which was not that difficult. You had to modify the order in which you performed things. At first, it was a little difficult or uncomfortable, but by the second or third paycheck, you hardly noticed. Congratulations.

This is a thought. Some of you can believe that $4,200 is not that much, but did you know it is enough for round-trip airfare (from Sydney to Phuket) plus living expenses for three months, yet Phuket is one of the most expensive countries in Southeast

Asia? Imagine enduring this for six months in the Philippines.

Most individuals work hard their entire lives only to "retire" destitute and rely on little savings or a (rapidly diminishing) government pension. They are forced to spend their golden years fighting chronic financial issues. If these individuals had consistently placed aside a small portion of their income for investing, they would have sufficient funds for a pleasant retirement.

The first rung on the path to riches is savings. The importance of savings in the school of wealth generation cannot be overstated. Instead of you saving what is left after your spending, the key to financial success and retiring wealthy is to spend what is left after saving—prosperous people save first and spend the remainder.

Many retire impoverished nowadays because they are large spenders rather than supersavers. Self-payment is what you receive from your savings. You sow the seed of your profits into the future to ensure your financial growth.

Remember that regardless of your life's accomplishments or wealth accumulated, you can end up retiring in abject poverty if you don't have savings and investments.

Savings are a very strong indicator of your plans. If you do not develop the practice of saving, you can live in poverty for the rest of your life. Not how much money you make, but what you can maintain matters the most.

Your savings provide for your future. The more you save, the greater your ability to purchase financial independence and live a life of pleasure and plenty. Do not put off saving until it is convenient. If so, you will have to wait forever.

Without savings, it is not easy to build wealth. Many individuals cite their earnings as the reason they do not save. The reality is that what matters is not your pay but rather your savings. Because what you rescue will be your salvation. Saving should be a requirement for everybody who wishes to retire wealthy and survive in a tough economy. Still, they ended up in poverty because they disregarded the notion of saving.

I am sure you have access to individuals who were once wealthy but are now living in abject poverty. They live with regrets. They neglected to save and invest for the future, so they now face poverty and deprivation.

Today, we are solely accountable for amassing a nest egg and ensuring it will sustain us during retirement. This can be a frightening duty but manageable if you approach retirement planning correctly. The earlier you start saving, the more you can amass.

If you save N5,000 per month for forty years at a return-on-investment rate of 25% per year, you can amass N1,8 billion. The actual savings of N5,000 each month for forty years amounts to N2,400,000. Finally, if you save N25,000 every month for ten years, you will accumulate N11.2 million from a total of N3 million.

THE FINEST MONEY-SAVING IDEAS OF ALL TIME.

At whatever point in history, certain money-saving strategies remain constant regardless of the status of the economy, prevailing fashions, unemployment, or interest rates. Some of you can be familiar with these concepts, while others may be completely unfamiliar. Whether or not you are familiar with these incredible secrets, using them in your life will be well worth your time.

The financial miracles they will do for you are assured. I urge you to implement them since anyone could transform your life! Small modifications can lead to tremendous results. Thus, adding one from eleven distinct locations will yield significant results. One plus one does equal two.

This list on preserving your hard-earned money in some straightforward ways. There is nothing here that cannot be performed daily.

1: Keeping track of your everyday expenditures.

Albert Einstein said, "It takes a genius to recognize the obvious." He meant that often the simplest things in life are the most potent, but because they are so basic, we tend to disregard them and not put them to use for us.

Keeping track of your everyday expenditures is one of the easiest yet most effective money-making strategies. Purchase a small notebook from a dollar store and bring it wherever you go. Record every dollar that you spend. It is that straightforward.

In just a few weeks, something magical will occur in your financial life if you follow these steps.

There is something tremendously powerful about recording your expenses on paper. It makes the flow of money in your life more tangible and precise.

It demonstrates simply and plainly where and why you are spending your money. Once you realize this, it becomes much simpler to manage your finances.

Not only have many people who have adopted this practice learned something about themselves that they never knew before, but they are often shocked. By analyzing their journal, a person can discover that they spent about $2,000 on a diet of soft drinks, snacks, and candy during the year!

Their annual salary is only $25,000, so they recognized that 8% of their income was being frittered away on something completely unnecessary. The individual gave up snacks and beverages and discovered they had enough money for a vacation the following year. Which would you select if you could pick between snacks and a trip?

The idea is that their daily cost diary helped them gain the perspective and clarity necessary to gain financial control. A basic spending log will give you control over your expenditures and, consequently, your financial life. There may be nothing standing between you and financial freedom than a 75-cent notebook and a ballpoint pen.

2: Stop running up debts!

We are all aware of the problems Uncle Sam has caused by spending more money than the government receives. It is known as debt spending. Do not deceive yourself. The same rules apply to you as they do to everyone else. These vile plastic cards may be the "American Way," but they are fearful.

Today, the average credit card borrower carries a debt of $8,000!

As many of you probably know, accumulating credit card debt is simple. This is psychological. Giving a credit card to a cashier differs from giving somebody a stack of green dollars. Would you hand over a handful of 10-dollar bills as effortlessly as a credit card? Most likely not!

Credit cards put people in debt and keep them there. Even for those with adequate earnings, paying off credit card debt is extraordinarily difficult. Make no mistake about it; credit card debt will drain your financial strength just as quickly as an open vein can drain your life force. Using a credit card by choice might rapidly become a necessity. Once that stage is reached, you are already in trouble.

There is no secret method to escape the credit card game. Today, you must take out a pair of scissors, cut your credit cards in half and start paying them back gradually. Always pay more than the minimum amount owed, even if it's only $10 extra.

Once you cease adding to the debt, even the smallest payments will accumulate over time. If you are patient and disciplined, you can overcome debt. After your cards have been canceled, you must adhere to a rigorous pay-as-you-go policy. Instead of buying now and paying later, you should save and wait until you have the whole cash to purchase.

Stopping credit-based spending is one of the most effective financial techniques available to everyone today. Why not accept and use this tool?

3: Sell your things.

That is true, and a large yard sale is long overdue. Search your home or apartment for any item you could sell at a flea market or yard sale that you do not need.

Perform an inventory. The truth is that most individuals are stunned by their possessions and the amount of money they have wasted on meaningless items. Why allow it to gather dust in your attic when you might earn interest on it in a savings account?

A garage sale is a wonderful way to clean up your home and provide a psychological boost that helps people regain control of their lives and finances. You can be $500, $1,000, or even $3,000 wealthier by the end of the week. In addition, you will have a feeling of starting over with a clean house.

4. A savings account will alleviate stress in your life.

Long ago, Benjamin Franklin stated, "A penny saved is a penny earned." Yes, it remains accurate and one of history's most effective money-making strategies.

Franklin's famous remark alludes to the difficulties of saving. It is not easy to save and simple to spend! You are aware! For this reason, every cent saved is genuinely earned, as retaining that money requires so much effort! But if you succeed, it will transform your life.

Imagine being in front of your bills instead of behind. When you are current on your bills, you gain control over your entire life. You sleep better at night. You are better able to generate new strategies to earn and conserve more money. Once you start to save, it spreads like wildfire.

Here are some money-saving tips:

Do not limit yourself to interest checking. Have a savings account that is more difficult to access than a checking account.

Keep your savings in a bank that is not on your typical route or perhaps even in a different city. Thus, you will not be tempted to use it each time you visit the bank to make a deposit.

Purchase short-term savings bonds with maturities between six months and one year. Thus, you will earn a greater interest rate while retaining access to your funds in case of genuine crises.

You should open the account under two names and require both withdrawal signatures if possible. Two persons can discuss each withdrawal and keep one another in check.

Once you receive your paycheck, deposit at least 5 percent into your savings account. You'll be pleasantly pleased by how much you've saved after just one year and feel wonderful about it.

5. Every day, visualize wealth and abundance.

Am I recommending you pursue some type of woo-woo mysticism to become a "money magnet"?

Maybe yes, maybe no! Call it a mind game, mysticism, or New Age nonsense, but the reality remains that behind every affluent man and woman is a positive outlook on money. Here is a quick demonstration:

(1) Person A, with a bad money mindset, has the following daily thoughts: "Jeez! $20 is difficult to come by. I work so hard and receive so little compensation. Money slips through my fingertips like water. How much money that you need to make to survive in the modern world is incredible.

With my meager income, I will never be able to afford a new car, but this job is still the best thing for me. Some people find it easy to make much money, but I am not one of them "ad infinitum.

(2) Person B, with a positive money attitude, has the following everyday thoughts: "If I work my tail off, I can get a raise next month, and I'll put fifty percent of the other earnings into a savings account.

There must be a hundred different ways I may earn extra money.

Money is not very difficult to earn if you work hard, control your expenditure, and save a little bit. This country has enough riches for everyone, and I can simply obtain my part and more "ad infinitum.

Okay. Who do you believe will have the greater chance of success?

Person A brings himself down with his ideas, whereas Person B gives himself a fighting chance.

Consider that having either negative or positive ideas incurs no expense. Therefore, why not think positively?

Much research has been conducted on the cognitive processes and mentalities of some of the world's wealthiest and most successful individuals. They all shared a favorable view of money and their ability to earn it.

6. Follow your passion, and the money will come to you.

I believe a book with that title exists. In any event, it is true. Many people live paycheck to paycheck and are poor despite working hard in their careers because they dislike their occupations.

If you dislike your job, you will negatively view money. Every morning, you will associate money with the awful sound of the alarm clock. Once you associate your source of money and income with drudgery, drudgery will dominate most of your life.

You should start organizing your escape immediately. The initial question to ask oneself is: "What would I be doing if money were no object? What do I enjoy doing most for enjoyment, and is it possible to get paid for it?"

Does this sound ridiculous? It is not. You are fighting against yourself if your work is not your play. You will eventually become exhausted and despise the world.

On the other hand, if you wake up each day excited, optimistic, and looking forward to what you will be doing - and making money at it - you will naturally progress toward doing more of what you love and making more money doing it.

If your desired career requires you to create your firm, do not let that deter you! It is considerably simpler than most individuals believe. It might profoundly change the course of your life.

7. You must organize yourself.

Being organized and productive impacts your income more than you could ever imagine. You cannot afford to be a slob if you wish to be wealthy. Consider the matter carefully. Suppose you are at your desk attempting to complete some work. You must locate the stapler, but because your office is so disorganized, it takes you fifteen minutes to do so.

You have just spent 15 unproductive minutes. Next, you must locate a file, which requires 20 minutes of paper searching. Another 20 minutes of watching television and searching for items might easily consume two to three hours towards the end of the day. The same holds for every type of employment.

How much time do auto mechanics spend searching for a nine-sixteenth wrench when they could have it at their fingertips?

Disorganized people continually lament at the end of the day, "I worked so hard yet got so little done!" Of course! You spent an entire day searching for Scotch tape.

In reality, time equals money. The more time you spend engaging in unproductive activities, the less time you spend making money. De-clutter your office. Organize the equipment shed. Get your paperwork in order. Consider each minute saved as a dollar in your pocket.

8. Create your own top ten list daily.

Regarding organization, you should sit down every morning with a cup of coffee and list the top ten tasks you want to do that day. Then arrange them in order of significance. Start at item 1 and proceed as quickly as possible down the list.

Without question, this is an effective method for getting work done. It will provide you with vast sums of money. Making money is all about movement, specifically forward mobility. According to the famed novelist Ayn Rand, the most crucial thing a person can do in a capitalist society is advance daily!

A list of your top ten priorities will ensure you do something daily. You cannot complete the full list daily, nor should you attempt to. Just do your best. You should be able to look at your list with pride, inspect the items that have been crossed off, and say, "I did it!" "That's what I accomplished today! I took action to improve my life and create wealth!"

Again, most of the wealthiest and most successful people in history have employed this strategy. You should join the club.

9. You must establish both short and long-term goals.

How can you expect to get somewhere if you do not know where you're going? It is basic but effective logic. When you have a target in the distant future that represents your goal, it might almost function as a magnet that pulls you toward it.

Setting reasonable yet challenging goals has repeatedly proven to be one of the most effective strategies for earning riches and success. It has been established in business training programs. It has been utilized repeatedly with success by innumerable persons.

Setting both short-term and long-term goals has the effect of laser-focusing your attention. It propels you towards greater and better things. It provides substance to what you are attempting to do, making what you want more genuine and likely to manifest in your life.

As you have likely heard, it's best to write down your short- and long-term goals and put them in your office and home. Every morning, you should start by reviewing your list of goals and compiling a Top 10 to-do list that will get you closer to your goals. Every night before you retire to sleep, you should evaluate your short-term and long-term goals and pledge to do everything you can to make them a reality.

Invest your funds and put them to work expanding themselves.

As stated previously, keeping money in a savings account is essential, but the 2.3% interest rates offered by most banks are insufficient to keep up with inflation.

You must do more than save your money — you must invest it. This includes financial instruments with extremely high rates of return, such as mutual funds, equities, and the riskier commodity markets.

A $5,000 investment in commodities can yield a return of $50,000 or 10 times the initial investment in just a few weeks. However, it is also possible to lose the entire investment. Invest your cash in a certificate with a long maturity (CD). They are 100% secure and offer a substantially higher return than standard savings accounts. Typically, you can obtain one with an interest rate of 4.5 to 5%.

In conclusion, you should allocate a percentage of your funds to high-yield or high-risk investment plans. This is the way to advance truly. 11th Outstanding Money Tip Have fun! This advice is included on my list because it is essential to your success.

You must enjoy yourself to be optimistic and remain optimistic about earning money. So, hurry up! Exit: laugh, clap your hands, and live! Enjoy yourself while raking in the bucks! The world awaits your arrival! Enjoy all you do, and you will achieve success."

I hope you have discovered many new ways to save your hard-earned money and enjoy life more. Remember that nothing presented in this four-part series is impossible. If you put this information to good use, you are guaranteed to gain from it and create wealth.

PART 2 – INVEST.

WHAT IS AN INVESTMENT?

The lack of comprehension of the rules governing the game of investing contributes to the failure of many people, some of whom perform fearfully. It is self-evident that you cannot win a game by breaking its rules. However, you must understand the rules before you can avoid breaking them.

Another reason investors fail is that they participate in the game without comprehending its rules. Deciphering the meaning of the word "investment" is essential.

What is an investment?

An investment is a revenue-producing asset. You must carefully notice every word in the definition since they are essential to comprehending the true meaning of investing.

According to the definition, there are two essential characteristics of an investment. Before a possession, item, or piece of property can be considered an investment, it must satisfy both criteria. Otherwise, it will not be considered an investment.

The first characteristic of an investment is that it is valued - that is, something that is important or beneficial.

Therefore, any possession, belonging, or property with no value is not an investment and cannot be one. According to this definition, a worthless, useless, or minor item, possession, or asset is not an investment. Every investment has a monetary value that can be quantified. That is, each investment has a monetary value.

The second characteristic of an investment is that it must generate income and be valuable.

Every investment has the ability, duty, responsibility, and role to generate wealth. This means it must be able to generate income for the owner or at least assist in generating revenue. This is an immutable characteristic of an investment.

No matter how valuable or priceless it may be, a possession, item, or property that cannot create revenue for its owner or at least assist the owner in creating income is not and can't be an investment. Moreover, any item that cannot fulfill these financial functions is not an investment, regardless of how pricey or costly it may be.

You should also consider a third investment feature strongly tied to the second feature discussed above. This will also assist you in determining if an asset is an investment.

The third characteristic of an investment is that an investment that does not create income or contribute to income generation saves money.

Such an investment prevents the owner from incurring some expenses he would have incurred in its absence, yet it may not be able to generate profits for the investor. In this manner, the investment creates money for the owner, although not strictly speaking. In other words, the investment generates money for the owner/investor.

Before a property qualifies as an investment, it must be able to create income or save money for the owner, in addition to being of high use and significance. It is essential to underline the second characteristic of an investment (i.e., an investment as being income-generating). This assertion is based on the premise that most individuals evaluate only the first factor when determining what constitutes an investment.

They view the investment as merely a value, even if the valuable consumes income. Typically, such a misunderstanding has severe long-term financial ramifications. Such individuals often make costly financial mistakes that cost fortunes throughout their lifetimes.

Perhaps, among the reasons for this misunderstanding is that it is tolerated in intellectual circles. In conventional educational institutions and academic publications, investments, often known as assets, relate to goods or properties in the context of financial studies.

Therefore, corporate organizations consider all their jewels and possessions assets, even if they do not generate money. This concept of investing is unacceptable among financially savvy individuals since it is inaccurate, deceitful, and misleading.

Consequently, some businesses mistakenly believe their liabilities to be their assets. Also, for this reason, some individuals perceive their liabilities to be their assets/investments.

Unfortunately, many people, especially financially illiterate, perceive non-profitable assets that eat their wages as investments. These individuals include their income-generating assets on the list of their investments. These individuals are financially illiterate. This is the reason why they have no financial future.

What financially knowledgeable people perceive as income-consuming assets, financial illiterates view as investments. This demonstrates the perception, logic, and mentality gap between financially knowledgeable and uninformed individuals. Financially intelligent individuals have a financial future, but financially illiterate individuals do not.

From the preceding statement, the first question you should ask yourself when investing is, "How valuable is the asset you wish to purchase with your money?" The better the investment, all else being equal, the greater the value (though, the higher the acquisition cost will likely be). The second consideration is, "How much revenue can it generate for you?"

If anything is valuable but does not generate revenue, then it is not (and can't be) an investment and can't provide money if it is not valuable. If you cannot affirmatively answer both questions, then what you do and obtain can't be considered investments. You can acquire a liability at best.

Individuals can save for retirement, their children's college education, or other financial goals by investing their money. Before making their first investment, novice investors must take the time to define their goals and learn some fundamental concepts of investing. Successful investment requires extensive research, dedication, and perseverance.

As starting investors generate income through investments, they will acquire a certain level of expertise. However, even the most experienced and competent investors face some danger. Start-up investors will be more successful if they can answer some fundamental investment questions.

How much capital do I require to invest?

A widespread misperception among novice investors is that they must have substantial capital to invest. Many investments can be made with as little as a few hundred or even a few thousand dollars.

The use of dividend reinvestment schemes or direct stock purchase options is one way to begin investing on a small scale. Investors may be able to invest in the stock options of a firm by paying a modest start-up fee, typically between $25 and $50, and making an initial investment. Once the money has accumulated, the investor can transfer them to a brokerage account where they can invest in larger quantities.

WHAT ARE THE MANY DIFFERENT FORMS OF INVESTING?

Once investors conclude that they have sufficient funds for an investment, the most challenging step is often determining where to invest. Many investment possibilities are available to investors; mutual funds, bonds, futures, and real estate are among the most common.

Mutual funds allow anyone to invest without having to "handle the investments themselves." Investors in mutual funds work with a professional portfolio manager. This manager invests in the market the pool of money contributed by many different investors.

The funds may be invested in closed-end or open-end funds. Closed funds distribute and sell a fixed number of shares to the public, whereas open-ended funds do not have a set number of shares.

The trader will reinvest the investor's funds in fresh shares. The shares are managed by a professional money manager trained to choose investments that would offer the investor the highest returns.

Exchange-traded funds - ETFs- are pools of investor capital invested similarly to mutual funds. However, because ETFs are meant to track specific indexes, and a large portion of their administration is automated, their maintenance expenses and fees are typically substantially cheaper.

When investors purchase bonds, they purchase a stake in a business or corporation. The corporations issue bonds, which are investor loans. In exchange, the company undertakes to pay back the investor at regular periods with interest.

Bonds can be a relatively solid investment option. Unless the company declares bankruptcy, it is very assured that the investor will receive at least a minimal amount of his investment back.

These interest payments at regular times can serve as a source of continuous income for retired couples and those seeking to develop a form of investment with consistent returns. Certain types of bonds may provide tax-exempt interest income.

Real Estate - When the moment is right, it may be a profitable investment but involves much work. Investing in a (REIT) or real estate investment trust is a simple way for investors to enter the real estate industry.

Investors become co-owners of the REIT's investments, such as shopping centers, parking garages, hotels, and other real estate projects. Because REITs pay no federal income tax in exchange for distributing 90 percent or more of their profits as dividends to stockholders, they often pay out significant cash dividends.

Purchasing homes, renovating them by fixing them or adding amenities and selling them for a profit, or renting the houses to tenants and obtaining a monthly income from rent payments are other ways to generate revenue through real estate investing.

Futures - Futures trading is the marketplace where buyers buy and sell futures contracts worldwide. Futures contracts are agreements to receive a product at a stated price at a future date.

Once the price is agreed upon, it is locked in for the next year, regardless of market fluctuations. Commodities, currencies, stock indexes, interest rates, and alternative investments such as economic indicators are typical futures markets. The advantages and hazards of this type of investment can be substantial. Therefore, only investors with the most experience should trade futures.

Should I diversify my investments or remain with one?

According to the vast majority of expert financial consultants, diversification is the cornerstone of a successful investment portfolio. Diversifying their investments reduces the danger that they will lose all their assets if a particular investment fails.

While it may be tempting to invest large quantities of money immediately, novice investors should weigh the possible return against the hazards they expose themselves to in the investment market.

Employing the services of a qualified investment advisor.

An investment advisor is a financial planner who can occasionally assist with all financial concerns. A professional investment advisor can offer novice investors the fundamental information required to create a portfolio. Some investment advisors are compensated based on a proportion of the managed assets' value, while others charge an hourly fee or are compensated on a commission basis.

The easiest way for investors to avoid these costs is to conduct research and start with mutual funds or ETFs supplied by trustworthy businesses.

HOW TO BECOME WEALTHY AS AN INVESTOR.

Investment is best defined as spending money, time, and effort into a business or other endeavor with the expectation of a return. It may include Real Estate, Mutual Funds, Stocks, and Foreign Exchange, among others. Regardless of the type of investment, there are guidelines and instructions for reaching achievement that, when followed, result in much better levels of success.

Before engaging in any type of investment, regardless of one's financial standing, it is vitally important to familiarize oneself with the rules and guidelines, given the elevated level of risk associated with most investments, to avoid becoming an object of pity as a result of a mistake caused by not following the rules.

The (SEC) or Securities and Exchange Commission of the United States, defines an individual as an Average Investor if they have an annual income of $200,000 or more, $300,000 or more as a couple, or a net worth of $1 Million or more.

This SEC regulation is intended to shield the average investor from some of the world's worst and riskiest investments. These investor requirements also insulate the average investor from some of the world's top investments, which is one of the primary reasons one must be just above the ordinary investor.

As millions of aspiring investors fall below the average investor, it would be unjust and depressing to continuously refer to Average and Rich Investors without mentioning Poor Investors whenever investment issues are discussed. After all, they both began from scratch.

A progressive transformation that transformed them into what they are now. Once there is life, there is hope for the average person and an abundance of investment prospects in the future.

Therefore, starting an investment with a small amount of accessible capital is strongly suggested for the poor investor, who would reach their goals with prudence, minimal effort, time, hope, faith, and patience.

An essential aspect of investing is one's mentality. The mental capacity to handle the challenging tasks involved with investments. Nothing worthwhile comes easy in life! Before going on a trip to invest, one must ask themselves some vital questions. These questions are:

- Am I truly committed to starting an investment?

- Which sort of investment is appropriate for me?

- How many funds do I need to initiate an investment?

- Should I invest alone or with others?

- What is my risk tolerance?

When a person correctly answers these questions and still wants to invest his money, he is qualified for the next level of investment success.

The sort of investment that best suits an individual relies entirely on the types of investments already available - Real Estate, Mutual Funds, Stocks, Foreign Exchange, etc. - the quantity of capital available to the individual and his or her particular interest in specific investment types. All the information guides him in determining the type of investment that best suits him.

Capital should not be a huge concern. Individuality and the nature of the investment determine the capital required to launch an enterprise. There are investments, stocks, in which one may invest with as little as a few cents. Consequently, money is almost meaningless when discussing penny stocks and should never deter individuals from investing their money.

Investing alone or with others is a completely personal decision. Each investment is present. As a novice, it is highly recommended that you invest together. Considering the inherent dangers in investments, which will always be divided, as it would be for the profit, among the investors in proportion to the amount invested by each, is an ideal starting point. However, investing alone is also advantageous.

Even more advantageous is if one can tolerate the dangers of single-person investments. The benefits from a solo investment will never be shared with anyone other than the sole investor, who will keep them all. Therefore, the decision is left up to the individual, taking into account suitability and convenience.

Even though a substantial level of risk is inherent in most investments, the greater the amount of capital spending, the greater the potential risks. Depending on one's investment strategy, the more capital spent, the greater the potential investment returns. It is a question of proportion. The possibility of becoming a wealthy, average, or poor investor is outside one's door.

This is the final step and leads toward a greater adjustment in a person's financial situation based on risk tolerance. With a bold step and rigorous respect for the rules and guidelines outlined in this section, success as an investor is certain.

HOW TO START INVESTING TODAY WITH THE MONEY YOU CURRENTLY SPEND.

Many people enter the job market following graduation and go headfirst into adulthood. The income from a job is immediately spent on liabilities, food, and entertainment — all essentials and luxuries of living.

This is commonly referred to as being in a "rat race." Every month is the same: income is received and expended. Once trapped, it is extremely difficult to escape but not impossible.

Now, the amount of money you earn at work depends on your ability to do a task or function and the amount of time you devote to it. Essentially, it is the exchange of time for money through a taught talent, but this can't continue forever, can it? What happens when you become too elderly to perform these work requirements?

Unfortunately, it lasts a very long time for some individuals. When people who do not invest in items that will generate income, whether or not they work, can no longer work, they will maintain their current standard of living.

Until most people obtain a career job with decent benefits (including a 401k), they invest their money seldom. Money is created and spent as quickly as earned, providing a person with the essentials and comforts of life at the time - and more - but not much for a happy future after employment income ceases.

At some point in their lives, everyone must confront the fact that work will not provide them with everything they desire or need, especially after retirement. Investing is something that is ideally learned early in life.

To comprehend the significance of investment, one must first understand what investing is. An investment is a one-time means of generating income. This work can sometimes be intensive and time-consuming, but it can give revenue for many years without requiring the same effort or time.

If you conduct extensive research to purchase a home for investment purposes, you will only need to conduct that study once. Once you purchase an investment, it will generate profits with minimal effort.

If you write a book and put it on a website to sell, you only need to write it once, and it will continue to generate revenue as long as it is available on the internet or in bookstores. If you examine a company's stock and select the ideal one, invest it; your money will start working and earning without your involvement.

These are merely straightforward investment examples that require some effort. If you know what you are doing, making money with investing is far simpler than making money through a job. The distinction between an investment and a job lies in the time and effort required to generate income.

The great thing about investing in the stock market (whether through conventional buy-and-hold-and-sell trading, 401(k) investing, or options) is that once you have learned the ropes, you can just carry on riding them, letting your money do the heavy lifting while you enjoy your life.

There is a MASSIVE obstacle that everyone must overcome before investing. Where do you get money to invest in your business? When living in a "rat race," one finally becomes trapped in an impossible circle that is extremely difficult to escape.

Not to worry! You have money; you simply do not realize it yet.

Regardless of the type of investment you intend to start, there are ways to start accumulating "money" by making a few adjustments to your lifestyle. It will begin to slowly but eventually transform into something you will not believe is conceivable.

A "Round Up" Savings Account is one relatively fast approach to accumulating investment funds. This account lets you save and accumulate funds based on your everyday spending.

You link your spending checking accounts or credit cards to your Round Up account, and with each transaction, this account rounds up to the nearest dollar. Not much effort, correct? This investment account takes care of the rest. It puts the difference into an investment platform that accelerates the growth of your funds.

For instance, if you paid $20.57 for an item, the total is rounded to $21.00. The rounded-up amount, or $0.43, is deposited into your account and distributed across multiple equities based on your account settings.

If you make 50 purchases from your checking account per month and round up each transaction by an average of $0.35, you will save $17.50 that month. That is a saving of $210.00 each year by rounding up purchases.

The value of the funds invested in this round-up account fluctuates with the stock market. At a 5% increase per year, the price will increase by $10.50. In addition, certain equities in which your funds are invested generate dividends automatically reinvested into your account.

It might not seem like much now, but it will continue to grow over time. This is an investment that can increase rather quickly if you continuously add to it. If you have extra funds you'd like to save each month, you can make other deposits to your account to help it grow even more quickly.

A Round Up Savings Account is merely a stepping stone to a higher level of investing, such as stock trading, options trading, a retirement investment account, real estate, or anything else you can invest to earn more money.

Once you have accumulated sufficient investing capital in your Round Up account, you can withdraw it at any time and use it to purchase assets (things that earn you money, as opposed to liabilities) or to invest in stocks to make even more money over time.

PART 3 - DEBT FREE.

The next essential step in your mentality to create wealth is to consider yourself debt-free. Since you cannot build wealth if your funds are eaten by debt, spending could be one of the leading reasons for stress and unhappiness in your life, especially if your debt continues to increase and your payments never seem to end.

While credit gives the instant joy we all crave, it robs you of the chance to build true, sustainable wealth, and once you allow yourself to incur debt, it is typically challenging to escape. It is easy to become buried in credit card interest rates and service costs, let alone other consumer loans!

But regardless of how much debt you have, there is still hope. Therefore, you must prioritize debt-free as quickly as possible and assess each credit offer critically. Another major step is to determine the monthly cost of your debt. As a result, you will know how much your debt costs monthly in interest and fees. You will be astounded by how enlightening this little activity is.

If you did not have debt, you could use the funds to generate wealth over time.

Therefore, it is imperative that you eliminate your debt as rapidly as feasible, and one of the most effective ways is to implement a debt reduction plan that you are committed to implementing with every pay cheque you receive.

Also, it would be beneficial if you had someone to whom you were accountable for your activities and debt reduction strategy, such as a trusted friend who shares your goal of becoming debt-free or a financial coach.

And if you have children, ensure that they are aware of your actions so that you can serve as a role model for them. Typically, children imitate their parents. Therefore, this would be an excellent moment to educate them on the detrimental effect of debt on wealth building. In addition, the Taking Control of Your Money Workbook is a valuable resource.

No doubt, spending money brings excitement and an emotional high. Still, you should never forget that every dollar you spend has the potential to jeopardize your financial future and wealth building, as opposed to increasing it.

Consequently, you should seek to maximize the return on every dollar spent. Because if you look after your dollars, the tens and twenties will look after themselves. When you consider it, nothing is more detrimental to your financial life than debt. Debt robs you of your hard-earned cash today and the wealth you can accumulate tomorrow.

Unfortunately, you are not alone if you believe that it is difficult to live without debt; we live in a society where debt is expected and thought inevitable, but have you ever imagined what life would be like without debt?

To be able to go to the post office at the end of the month without fear of debts awaiting you! Or the ability to answer the phone without being concerned about who is on the other end.

While others may believe that debt-free life is a myth and that it is acceptable to be financially stressed, wouldn't it be amazing if this were not your norm? Like the lepers in 2 Kings 7, you can now decide that you will not continue to accept the current quo and will instead do something radical: become debt-free.

You will feel changes in every part of your life as a result of this one change:

- Without consumer debt, life is significantly easier from a financial standpoint.
- You will feel emotionally relieved because a very great burden has been removed from your shoulders.
- Physically, it is healthier to be debt-free, as mental tension often shows in physical ailments.

- Following God's plan for your life will be easier without consumer debt.
- Without consumer debt, you will have enormous flexibility.

Have you ever thought about the definition of the word "consume"? It means "to utterly consume" or "to demolish." Consumer debt is any debt gotten for products that will degrade in value over time, such as credit card, furniture, travel, apparel, and automobile debt.

While your mortgage may not be listed now, you can eliminate this debt once you no longer have to make these other payments.

But continue to be a consumer. You will never be able to attain financial independence, as "living debt-free" is one of the most essential steps toward prudent money management and the quickest route to wealth accumulation.

The good news is that it is feasible to eliminate this debt! And once you are debt-free, it is possible to remain debt-free for the rest of your life. However, the amount of time and work required depends on the amount of debt you have.

As with breaking any habit, escaping debt will necessitate certain behavioral and cognitive adjustments. This is essential since it is all too common for people who find a way to quickly get out of debt to end up back in debt because while their financial situation changed, their values did not. Remember that it will take some time, and revisions will be necessary.

Since you are contemplating a change, why do you wish to eliminate your debt? What is your motive? Always be aware of why you are making a change, as this will serve as your inspiration during difficult moments.

Once you are debt-free, what financial goals would you like to achieve?

Do you have sufficient funds for peace of mind? (Money to pay for life's unforeseen calamities, such as illness, car difficulty, and home maintenance.

Would you rather save for a car or a housing down payment?

Which Religious or Nonprofit Effort Would You Like to Support?

Keep these motives and goals in mind since remembering your goals will help you stay on track.

Lastly, do you realize how you get into debt?

The answer to this question is essential because it allows you to comprehend the cause of your debt. As is typically the case, divorce, business failure, or simply living over my means are the causes of my debt. Unemployment, medical issues, etc., may have caused your debt.

Now that you understand how you got into debt, you must choose why you want to get out and what you will do when you do. Here are nine strategies for permanently emancipating yourself from consumer debt.

Make an undertaking.

Write Your Commitment Down. There is something quite potent about making a promise. Once you have made a promise, you must put it in writing, sign it, and date it. Then, take it a step further by sharing it with a trusted friend or close relative and asking them to help you stay accountable to your debt-free goal.

Determine where you currently are.

You must clearly understand where you are and how much you owe to reach your destination. Include the total amount owed, the minimum monthly payment, and each creditor's interest rate.

Prioritize.

Prioritize your debt by assigning a 1 to the lowest balance, a 2 to the next highest, and so on. For loans with comparable sums, the higher interest rate should be prioritized.

Establish a spending plan.

The key to eliminating debt is making payments above the minimum required. Your spending plan and money management abilities will assist you in locating more funds to apply to your debt.

Simply Do It.

Stop talking and start acting. Remember that knowledge is not power; only the application of information creates power! Pay off the smallest loan balance first. Once that loan is paid off, roll the whole payment amount into the next bill and the next until you are debt-free.

Keep Going.

You will face obstacles, but you should not let them stop you. Focus on your goal and keep going forward.

Save some cash.

Before you start, have at least one month's worth of living expenses in peace of mind account.

Be a good steward.

God will establish your plan if you live up to your commitment to your local church.

The sooner you take drastic action and become debt-free as quickly as possible, the more time you will have to live a prosperous and pleasant life!

HOW TO UNDERSTAND THE PSYCHOLOGY OF DEBT AND GET OUT OF DEBT.

All wealth creation and life success require a strategy, be it an investment strategy, a tax strategy, a finance strategy, a loan strategy, a diversification strategy, or an income strategy, among others. This involves a debt reduction strategy, of course.

There are a few ways to approach this from a debt reduction plan; let us cover a few of them now.

How to get started, and what to do.

A few essential tasks must be performed for every loan that must be repaid.

1. Find other cash flow to pay more than the minimum sum on one debt. Take the time to assess your financial status and determine where and how your money flows.

2. Call your utility, insurance, communication, and lending companies and negotiate a better price with each one. You would be astonished at how often a better offer can be gotten by simply asking! A better deal might be in the form of a cheaper interest rate, a longer payment period, a different payment method, or anything else. Determine what you would ideally need to pay off your debt, write it down and ask for it.

3. Establish an order of debt payback - I will elaborate on this below.

Your debt repayment ranking.

Deal with the immediate.

It seems obvious that certain debts are more urgent than others; if debt collectors are pursuing you, ignoring the bill and hoping it goes away would not help. Clearly, you must take care of these first while preserving the others to avoid accumulating charges, preserve your credit history and, most importantly, preserve your sanity.

We end ourselves in a constant reactive state that requires us to focus on constantly putting out fires rather than on the most important aspects of our lives, which is not a pleasant experience.

Plan to address the most pressing bills first or, even better, call your creditor and negotiate the terms of the debt to make it "non-urgent," allowing you to address all obligations equally subsequently.

4. The highest priority first.

From a purely financial standpoint, it is always advisable to eliminate the debt with the highest interest rate first, as this is where you will save the most money. Start with the debt having the highest interest rate, pay the bare minimum on all other bills, and focus on these first because they are the most expensive.

Prioritize your smallest debt first to liberate your thoughts.

Previously, I mentioned that focusing on the debt with the highest interest rate is the most effective financial plan for eliminating debt. However, there is also a psychological component that can have an equal impact on your capacity to reduce your debt completely, particularly when you have multiple debts and a large amount of them; it can feel like an impossible and unachievable task and put us in a state of feeling helpless, which is not a very resourceful state to operate from.

Therefore, the psychological state you need to be in is also essential in addition to the financial strategy behind debt reduction. You get momentum when prioritizing eliminating your obligations from lowest balance to highest. When you start crossing off various debts, you can observe your plan's tangible benefits and success.

Momentum is a highly potent force. Progress produces momentum, momentum boosts dedication, and things suddenly start happening faster when you are on a roll. Your debt becomes less like a burden and more like a task to conquer and overcome, and you acquire the confidence that you can achieve your goals. Therefore, once the debt has been paid off, use this momentum to create wealth in the future.

Your chosen order will depend greatly on who you are and how well you comprehend your personality, motivation, and dedication. Working with hundreds of customers to reduce their debt and put them on the path to wealth creation has shown me that both are equally effective.

5. Snowflake it.

This is a straightforward yet highly successful idea. We are concentrating on making minimal payments on most of your bills and focusing on just one. Once the first loan is paid off, you must take the minimum payment you were making plus any other funds you had pledged and focus on your second priority bill.

Once this is paid off, apply everything from the first two debts plus any extra cashflow to the third debt until all debts are paid off. Because you continue to roll your minimum payments down the line of loans, this generates a snowball effect that rapidly reduces your balance.

You can also find Time to Take Charge of Your Finances interesting.

1. Treat your finances as a business.

After completing these steps, you must ensure that you never fall into the debt trap again and, more significantly, move on to wealth creation. Unfortunately, most people only manage their finances when there are bills to pay, emergency problems, or deep debt.

However, if you had spent time up front being initiative-taking about managing your finances, you probably would not be in this scenario in the first place. Start being proactive with your financial management immediately and manage your financial life as if it were a business; profitability is the cornerstone of any successful business.

Determine where you are right now. Create an income statement and balance sheet for your life. What are your debts? What resources? What is your incoming and outgoing cash flow? Establish a budget that will provide a weekly profit.

2. Track your spending for a few weeks (preferably four), get a small notepad and carry it everywhere,

download some smart mobile applications, or link a spending tracker to your bank accounts. There are some remarkable tools available.

This will provide you with immense clarity on your current financial situation and where your money is going and hold you accountable each time you pull out your wallet or purse to spend money. You will start to reconsider every buy.

3. Determine your intended destination. When you have a strong purpose and set of goals behind your wealth creation and why you want to build wealth in your life, your dedication to keeping true to your mission and goals is extremely powerful.

4. Develop a financial and investment plan - Start by reducing your bad debt and develop a plan for accumulating wealth and investing in growth assets. Get a coach if you are unsure of how to proceed, someone who can point you in the proper direction. If you hire the correct coach, you should receive a considerably better return on investment than the expense of hiring that individual.

5. Also, a financial planner is not necessarily competent coach or has ever amassed wealth for themselves but believes they can still teach it. Focus on outcomes, not qualifications. Qualifications are simple, but results are extremely unusual.

6. If you have a spending problem, place post-it notes with the question "do you need this?" on your credit card. Give yourself weekly pocket money and leave your credit cards at home. The aim is to prepare for possible obstacles and be honest about your strengths and limitations to devise countermeasures.

7. Schedule periodic review sessions. One of the most powerful habits you can create is a wealth night, time set aside once a week where you purposefully manage your money and review your outcomes - when I did this in my life. The feedback I have received from many clients I have put on this habit is that they feel in control of their finances for the first time rather than constantly feeling at the mercy of their money.

BAD DEBT CAN RUIN YOUR WEALTH.

Bad Debt can shackle you and halt your efforts to build riches. One of the most common mistakes real estate investors make is taking on too much bad debt - remember, this is debt that does not generate income or has an interest that is not tax deductible!

When you apply for a new loan to purchase an investment property, the amount of your income required to service your bad debt is subtracted from your overall income, which is then used to determine how much you can borrow.

Your borrowing capacity will be reduced due to your bad debt; the exact amount will depend on how much bad debt you have. Most people are unaware of how detrimental poor debt may be to their ability to borrow.

How can you expect a lender to advance you money to create an investment property if your only assets are credit card bills, personal loan statements, and a hefty mortgage on your residence?

I do not always comprehend how people can borrow up to their credit limit to overcapitalize their property, leaving little for the future. They max out their bad debt, make monthly minimum payments, and wonder why banks will not give them extra money to purchase an investment property!

I am aware that we have been raised in a world where borrowing money, especially bad debt, is an accepted practice, and it appears that this mindset is being passed down from generation to generation. This mentality has spawned many bad debt borrowing programs that allow individuals to borrow without interest and repayment for up to four years.

Statistics reveal that most individuals do not pay by the due date and, as a result, incur exorbitant interest rates. If you envision retiring at a young age, lounging in a deck chair, enjoying life, and playing golf, you should exclude the bad debt from your investment calculations.

Paying off bad debt is a straightforward approach that should be taught to everyone. The greater your bad debt, the more you are compelled to work to pay it off. You are less pressured to earn more if you have fewer bad debts.

YOUR STRATEGY FOR REDUCING DEBT.

First, you must construct and complete a Budget to determine how much extra cash you can allocate each week toward paying off the bad debt. You must continue making monthly payments on all your loans while paying down the balance on one.

A basic scenario:

- Personal Loan: $190.00 monthly payment
- Credit Card: monthly $280.00
- Loan for a Boat: $310.00 monthly
- Auto Loan: $750.00 monthly.

The plan is to take your smallest bad debt and boost the monthly payment by at least $50. Therefore, you pay $240.00 monthly on your loan until it is repaid.

Then you put the $240 you no longer spend on your loan into your next lowest bad debt, your credit card. Your new credit card payment amount is now $520.00.

Apply this method to each delinquent bill until you are DEBT-FREE.

Managing your finances requires discipline, but it can be incredibly rewarding.

The secret to an earlier and more prosperous retirement is having no bad debt and just good debt. Good debt generates money and/or attracts tax-deductible interest. The ATO permits you to balance the property expenses against your own earned income and the revenue from the investment property, allowing you to effectively pay less tax than you would ordinarily be required to.

The added benefit that generates true wealth is the property's capital appreciation over time. When this method is repeatedly balanced, the results are simply stunning.

You can raise the value of residential property by repair, subdivision, and other value-added activities, which is one of its chief advantages. You can also obtain a discount through research and bargaining.

Most real estate investors cannot afford the time or lack the knowledge to manage their properties. They generate income from other sources; real estate is merely a vehicle for storing and growing their income from other sources. There are many ways to accelerate money through real estate, but it depends on your willingness and ability to work.

A relatively small proportion of real estate investors work hard on their properties; some even abandon their careers and enterprises to focus on them. Depending on the type of investor you are, you will evaluate your properties following your specific requirements.

The quality of an investment property can be determined by how well it satisfies the investor's needs at a given time; hence, property performance is a subjective measurement for the investor and has minimal relevance for others.

Wealth development is mostly independent of external market conditions, a self-propelled process. People often attempt to buy low and sell high, but most of us can never perfect this timing. The optimal moment to purchase is whenever you are financially prepared; it is more important that you be prepared than that others are prepared for you.

CONVERTING DEBT TO WEALTH.

Step 1 - Get A Clear Picture Of Your Current Situation.

Irritate Yourself. If you are going to make the necessary changes to your financial structure, you must become extremely unsettled. I adore how Tony Robbins discusses it. He discusses weight loss but instructs individuals to undress, stand in front of a mirror, and examine their rear ends.

To accomplish this, you must have a clear understanding of your debt. Write it out in detail. On a piece of paper, record all your debts, not only the monthly payments but also the balances. If you own a home, you can remove it from the list for now. The house can be taken care of later, as it is almost always the most expensive item and will be paid off last.

Step 2 - Start Monitoring Your Spending.

Obtain a spiral notepad that you can always carry with you. Record EVERY cost you incur, EVERY dollar you spend, EVERYTHING! Once again, you must identify where the leaks are to correct your spending. People who keep a food journal are 77% more likely to lose weight while dieting than those who do not. The same applies to Debt Reduction. Always keep your journal on you.

Creating a "Is It Worth It?" sheet is another mental trick. These are useful since they reveal the cost of current expenditures. If you desire, you can construct your own. All you need to do is compile a list of products you enjoy purchasing, their prices, and the value of that money in one year, five years, ten years, and twenty-five years if invested at 8 to 10 percent each year.

Ten years from now, a cup of coffee at Starbucks may cost you hundreds, and a night out on the town could cost you $50,000. I can at least make an informed decision when I know the expense.

Step 3: Find an Accountability Partner.

There is no better way to boost your success than having a partner to hold you accountable. Ask a friend to analyze your numbers and discuss your journal, spending, etc., with you once a week or once a month (a week is preferable, but it depends on your friend).

Ensure kids be aware that it is their responsibility to hold you accountable and that they must ask difficult questions when you are spending more than you should. That is their purpose for being there. When you are struggling, you should investigate the causes, ask for strategies to help you achieve, and receive assistance in establishing procedures.

Step 4: Stop Using Credit Cards!

You have heard that using a credit card positively affects your credit score. I would rather be debt-free, credit-card-free, and have thousands of dollars in the bank every month, so I never need to utilize credit! Does it matter if you can never build the wealth you desire but have excellent credit?

Whenever feasible, cease using credit cards entirely. If you are having trouble, place your card in a plastic bag, place the bag in a paper cup, fill the cup with water and freeze the card. If you truly need that card, you must work hard to retrieve it. Do not heat the card in the microwave to melt the ice; the card will be damaged.

Step 5: Find Methods of Earning Extra Money.

More funds will facilitate immediate debt reduction. This could be accomplished by selling items on eBay, holding a garage sale, posting items for sale on Craigslist, or engaging in online endeavors. Regardless of the method you choose, you must take action. Without action, no other funds exist.

Step 6: Pay down the smallest loan first.

Many individuals advise you to eliminate the debt with the greatest interest rate. I believe that everyone with debt must first feel successful! Even if it costs you another $10 to $50 in interest, it is essential to generate a sense of accomplishment so that you will continue your efforts.

There are many ways to accomplish this. Some are effective. Others are merely a gimmick that provides no explanation and leaves you in a worse position than before! Those should unquestionably be avoided at all costs! However, you must take action! I have discovered one that surpasses all others in terms of user-friendliness, comprehension, and practical application.

PART 4 – PATIENCE.

WHAT DOES IT COST YOU TO DEVELOP PATIENCE?

To tell you the truth, that is a fairly expensive lesson. It will take much time and effort to perfect these abilities. In addition, consistency in one's actions and tenacity in the process is essential to developing patience.

The process of acquiring patience requires a huge lot of time, work, and energy. However, greater sacrifices yield greater rewards and accomplishments. Humans constantly seek instant gratification in all aspects of life: immediate profit schemes, instant cash, and instant noodles. In our view, we are continually searching for fast gratification.

We often fail to perceive and acknowledge that developing patience necessitates acquiring essential skills and knowledge for growing our consciousness and understanding of ourselves and others. In reality, all they require is time and patience.

No, I am not talking in riddles. I am simply telling the truth. Just picture this. How can one gain patience if they are not patient during learning?

Consequently, I believe that to acquire the "secrets" of patience properly, you must obtain new insights and knowledge of the rewards that excellent patience may provide.

You have undoubtedly heard that patience is a virtue. Yes, if viewed from the appropriate perspective. Overall, one should never use patience as an excuse to delay or as a "reason" to "wait for the proper moment."

Thus, "patience is a virtue" has been extensively misapplied, particularly among procrastinators. It has been dubbed the quote of the lazy man. Patience remains a virtue and will continue to be a virtue. You only need to possess the proper disposition and awareness of patience.

With a positive outlook and an understanding of the benefits of patience, you will be in a much better position to acquire patience. Learning patience is necessary for success, as most successful individuals preach.

With patience, you learn to appreciate the process and the journey rather than focusing just on the outcome. Contrary to widely held belief, a person's happiness is not determined by the number of accomplishments he or she achieves.

Instead, happiness is measured by how many times an individual has picked himself up after each fall. The amount of "battle scars judge it" one has acquired along the path to achievement. If you are patient, you will be given the skills and ability to transform all setbacks into victories and the willingness to lose minor battles to win the larger war.

Also, with patience comes trust and the realization that there are no true failures in life unless they are acknowledged.

Now, it may be true that we all experience temporary setbacks along the way. Still, it is also because of these temporary defeats that we learn more effective methods and tactics that we can utilize to win future significant fights in life.

Those who merely wait will not be rewarded. Instead, it attracts individuals who continually invest time, energy, and effort into cultivating patience and taking massive corrective action.

HOW TO GO FROM BEING DESTITUTE TO BEING RICH.

To attract prosperity, one must first believe they deserve it; otherwise, they may block their path with feelings of inadequacy and anxiety. It is not sufficient to covet money; one must believe one deserves it. This is one of the secrets to achieving financial success.

People conditioned to believe that their race, socioeconomic background, surroundings, or religion prevent them from acquiring riches find it challenging to do so. Decades of conditioning from discrimination might have a negative impact. In many instances, the lack of exposure to what money gives hampered economically disadvantaged individuals' educational, job and lifestyle options.

Thankfully, some people surmounted the harsh situations with pure determination and determinism. When this inferiority complex is thoroughly ingrained, it can be eradicated using counter-mind conditioning activities that penetrate the conscious and the subconscious minds.

MONEY HAS AN ENERGY FIELD.

Money attracts money in both the spiritual and physical realms. Money has its energy field and must be balanced with its subtle vibrations to attract it. In the same way, love attracts love, and fear draws fear.

Therefore, if you do not feel deserving or truly believe you can have it, you won't attract it. If you feel worthy to a small degree, your encounters with money may be fleeting and insignificant. You seem incapable of maintaining the prosperity channel.

Affirmations and/or supraliminal mind conditioning exercises are a wonderful starting point for establishing a more solid connection to your mental state of worthiness and ability to attract riches into your life.

From a religious perspective, specific biblical scriptures, old spiritual literature, prayers, psalms, and affirmations lend themselves to positive mental transformation and can be extremely effective when said daily.

Mind conditioning exercises are an alternative solution. It is the practice of changing negative thought patterns with positive ones to achieve desired outcomes. A positive thought must replace every negative idea that is eliminated.

FEEDING THE CREATIVE STRATUM.

God created the heavens and earth at the start of time. Now, the earth was void and formless; darkness covered the deep surface, and God's Spirit hovered over the waters

Before everything was, there was a concept. Imagination is the mental creation of visions of desired physical manifestation. It plays an essential role in the creative process since it forces a thought form from an idea to an actual substance.

Many legends make symbolic references to this, including Aladdin's Lamp, Biblical Manna, Peter Pan, and The Wizard of Oz. It is all about visualization and imagination.

How does one direct the imagination?

It can be accomplished by working to actualize the imagined concept. Imagine, consider, and discover a way to bring it to life through the use of images to illustrate the idea.

If you desire a luxury vehicle, you should visit a car dealership and test-drive one to get a feel for it and an authentic experience. If you desire a new home, go on house tours, and photograph the residences to identify your ideal property.

The goal is to bridge the gap between your thoughts and the real world. Through the power of one's imagination, the world can be transformed into one's dreams. I've done it before, so that you can do it too. I was able to get a car, a digital piano, a house, and a fantastic income through the employment of my imagination.

BRINGING YOUR IDEAS INTO BEING.

In life, we are often presented with possibilities to acquire a fortune, but we fail to seize them. Occasionally, these opportunities appear unappetizing, and we dismiss them because they do not fit our life's plan.

Those opportunities attired in enticing hues, alluring stature, and amusing forms are more readily accepted but are not always the greatest choices. Wealth opportunities often present themselves, but it is up to us to open the door. We unlock the door using the key. GRATITUDE! What is the secret?

Our desires, thoughts, and dreams are like small magnets that attract life experiences and possibilities. The bigger the passion, the quicker the opportunity will present itself, and the better it will correspond to our ideal desires.

Once an opportunity presents itself, we must open the door by accepting it with thankfulness and respect. The greater our appreciation, the more favorable the outcome of the Opportunity.

Few individuals truly comprehend the power of gratitude. They believe that gratitude merely expresses gratitude, but it is so much more—it results in action. Positive Action! The attitude of gratitude keeps us modest and in the "Law of Reciprocity" pattern of giving and receiving.

The "Law of Reciprocity" is a "give and take" factor that must be respected to distribute prosperity in full measure. This law is often mentioned in the Bible and other spiritual traditions.

Give, and you shall receive. A measure pressed, shaken, and running over will be dumped into your lap. Because according to the measure you employ, it will be measured to you. Even though these scriptures are considered part of Christianity's spiritual teachings, there is little doubt that they pertain to a Law that operates in the lives of everyone, regardless of religion, creed, or race. Chaos ensues when this Law is disregarded in our daily lives.

When we are not grateful for what we receive and don't reciprocate in some way, our soil or mind becomes fallow and the seeds we plant there eventually wither and die. Where there is no giving or friendly spirit toward humans, the path to prosperity can and will narrow. This spirit of generosity can take the shape of service, monetary contributions, lovingkindness, wisdom, and more.

Giving money to a cause you care so much about, volunteering at a non-profit event, mowing someone's lawn, delivering meals to a senior citizen, giving a friend a ride home, donating items to Goodwill, etc., are examples of such actions. On a Sunday evening, while enjoying supper and a great discussion, a member of our group revealed that he was unemployed and lacked funds for his next meal.

This talk resulted in this unemployed man receiving a job application from a buddy, who then submitted it at the workplace. The unemployed man was hired, and the person who submitted his application was promoted.

This is an example of the law of reciprocity, and there is little doubt that appreciation surrounds us with the energy of love, kindness, care, compassion, patience, and generosity. In this sense, prosperity also leads to excellent health and happiness.

Gratitude is Powerful and the key to unlocking the doors to prosperity and attracting possibilities that will clothe your needs and desires with substance. If you pay your debts with delight rather than hatred, they will be paid off faster. If you want more money in your life, you must become more grateful and demonstrate it in the ways outlined above.

If you want a new home, clean and beautify the one you have, and you will be given a superior one. If you desire a better job, find a way to love your current one and do outstanding work where you are, and you will be awarded a promotion (maybe even a new promotion).

If you are unemployed, spend some time helping at a non-profit organization; a job will appear. You would be shocked at how Gratitude can propel and bring your dreams to reality! Make it happen! Be Grateful!

WHY PATIENCE IS THE CRITICAL SUCCESS ELEMENT.

You desire prosperity and financial independence, correct? And you want it as soon as possible, particularly if, like many people, you are suffering from debts and obligations, worrying if your work is secure, and wishing you had a little extra for indulgences and relaxation. You have struggled for years, and now it would be nice to reap the rewards of your efforts.

Most people seeking financial independence believe it will arrive quickly and without difficulty. They observe someone who achieved achievement "overnight." they look at someone who is financially successful today but forget all the effort that person spent building their financial independence in the past.

This erroneous perception leads many people to believe that financial success — or success in any other aspect of life — may be theirs by tomorrow or, at the latest, by the end of the month.

However, as Napoleon Hill stated, you must learn the three main success elements of patience, persistence, and perspiration, which he regarded as an unbeatable success combination.

I want everything, and I want it RIGHT NOW!

Instant pleasure has become the norm in our society. Young people are notorious for expecting their every whim and wish to be fulfilled quickly. The media has convinced people that their lives will never be the same if they do not immediately get the newest designer item.

Financial organizations have also contributed by making credit readily available to credit-worthy individuals and others who are likely to struggle to maintain an excessive lifestyle. It appears that patience is no longer a virtue.

People like Edwin C. Barnes worked for Thomas Edison in a menial capacity while patiently awaiting the opportunity to become Edison's business partner. Similarly, Henry Ford waited patiently as his engineers worked to build the V-8 motor, which made him a fortune. Without perseverance, neither would have been successful.

Successful individuals are reluctant to change their minds once a decision has been taken. If you abruptly change your plans in the middle of their execution, you will never know what might have transpired. Sticking with your decision rather than changing your mind provides you time to let things play out so that you can examine the consequences of your actions with precision.

Persistence is the ability to persevere with a task to completion rather than giving up when things don't go your way quickly. The key to success in sales is getting yourself in front of a sufficient number of individuals who choose to purchase what you're selling. If many people have declined to purchase, placing yourself in front of the next potential customer can be difficult.

You convince yourself that there is no purpose because you will only be disappointed again, or perhaps you question whether your goods are worth purchasing. Negatives accumulate, forming a mental mountain that must be scaled to reach the next opportunity.

The major way to get through this is to continue doing what you're doing: be tenacious. Put on a grin, pick up the phone, knock on the neighbor's door, or whatever. The next individual you speak with could be the key to your success, but if you are not persistent, you can walk away instead of approaching them.

Form a habit to overcome a lack of perseverance. New endeavors or endeavors in which you have less self-confidence necessitate persistence more than others. Here, it is even simpler for negative thoughts and influences to take hold.

Stop worrying about the outcome and simply get started. If things do not go your way, it's a great opportunity to learn, and when they do go your way, those happy emotions will reaffirm the value of persistence.

10% Inspiration, 90% Perspiration.

Behind every successful person is a lot of unrecognized effort, especially by their critics. Thomas Edison failed many times before creating a functional light bulb. Successful athletes spend many hours perfecting their motions to make their performance in competition appear effortless. Reality television demonstrates that while skill is necessary, perseverance ultimately determines success or failure.

Anyone who has attained financial independence has done it via constant effort. They discovered a burning desire, utilized imaginative creativity to construct an orderly plan, then implemented the planned day after day until their 'instant' achievement began to appear.

Early accomplishments were celebrated as milestones, not the destination. Reversals were viewed as learning opportunities: modify plans and reevaluate techniques, not as reasons to give up.

Physical, mental, or both labor is the only sure route to achieving long-term financial independence. To achieve success, you should be willing to pay the price by cultivating and using the three most important success factors: patience, persistence, and perspiration.

THE FORMULA FOR WEALTH THAT CAN NEVER FAIL

How can I make a stable income and stop relying on others? This topic has often recurred in my interactions with many of my readers over the past year.

Every time someone asks me this question, it makes me ponder. I reverse the question and ask, "Is there a strategy for creating riches that can't fail? If there is a formula, what is it? How complicated is it? Can virtually anyone who is determined accomplish it?"

After months of intense contemplation and thorough investigation, I have the answers to these concerns. Yes, there is a strategy for creating wealth that can never fail! Before I describe the formula, let me briefly define the term "formula," as it is essential to your grasp of what I am trying to convey.

According to one online dictionary, a formula is a predetermined form of words, such as announcing or declaring something definitively or authoritatively, suggesting a procedure to be followed, or prescribing the use. In other words, it is accomplishing anything permanent or usual; a rule or principle, a recipe or prescription.

This definition suggests that a wealth development formula is a collection of guidelines or recipes. What, then, is the formula? It is a four-step method that, when integrated, allows you to generate riches.

Below are the four sections:

- Make God the cornerstone.

- Find a way to start making real income consistently and have the self-control never to spend it all.

- Master the art of receiving recurring payments for your services.

- Concentrate solely on steps 1, 2, and 3 by continually identifying ways to improve performance.

This is the equation. Now, let us dissect it. The first section is straightforward, correct? This means that you must choose to align yourself with what GOD says. That indicates you must be aware of what God has said and be able to align yourself with it.

The greatest method to accomplish this is to become a diligent student of the Word of GOD. You will establish a firm basis for wealth production as you understand its teachings and become dedicated to carrying them out.

For instance, if your GOD is the same as the one I serve, you will be a devoted hearer and doer of what GOD has said, as recorded in the Bible. A devout and enthusiastic practitioner of the Word is a certain prospect for lasting wealth.

This individual cannot fail to achieve overall success. This is how the Bible validates the claim: "Don't let this Book of the Law leave your lips; think on it day and night so that you will be cautious to follow all of its instructions. Then you will experience prosperity and success." Joshua 1:8.

This should cause you to rejoice if you are a doer and hearer of the Word. Why? You have become a doer because you have just heard Him say it, and if you now go forward and do what the Word says, you are no longer a hearer.

Then you will be eligible for what the Bible has promised. My GOD will never deny His existence. He will carry out everything He has stated in His Word. Nothing is impossible for Him.

The second part of the strategy is finding a technique to make real revenue consistently and never spend all your earnings. Typically, this doesn't mean income from a dream job or a top-tier profession. We are discussing a person who is likely unemployed, has no idea where their next meal will come from, or whose monthly income is "nothing to write home about."

The temptation for those in this condition is to become so disillusioned and discouraged that they choose to end their lives.

I must acknowledge that this is an extremely difficult position. You will not only regain your footing if you do what I am going to suggest but you will also be liberated from the chains of poverty. To overcome this obstacle, simply get up and identify a meaningful service you can do for someone in exchange for compensation and be sure that whatever it is is legitimate.

Then, when this effort starts to yield some revenue, take the next step and discipline yourself not to spend all your profits, regardless of how small they may be. This is a critical component of the recipe for creating riches.

Most people do not pass this stage. Either they remain in the menial job that provides them with a consistent income, or they see the money they earn with contempt instead of thanking God for it.

But if you get how this formula operates, your mindset will change. You will first recognize that this is a brief phase in your life. It's not a location where you want to spend too much time. The only goal here is to have enough money flowing in to give you some food to eat [not necessarily a satisfying meal regularly] and some to invest in personal growth.

Regarding your investment in self-improvement, choose carefully. The greatest strategy is to acquire the expertise you can master very well and use to benefit others. Here is a secret I would like you to discover.

For instance, you know for certain tasks that, individuals and businesses will always pay others to perform them. Choose one of these activities you enjoy, get proficient at, and strive to be the best provider of that service.

Before I explain the third component of this formula, I want to emphasize something else. Earlier, I cautioned you about the peril of becoming ungrateful for the minimal revenue you gain from performing menial tasks in the second step of the procedure. If you have the self-control to accomplish this, you are halfway out of poverty.

You should be quite cautious about it. If you allow a lack of thankfulness to seep into your heart, it will consume you, preventing you from engaging in self-improvement. If you allow this to occur, you will be in danger. So be cautious!

Okay, you have now passed the first perilous obstacle, where many fail. In the third half of the formula, your goal is to improve your expertise to be repeatedly paid for your service.

What does this mean?

Remember that you now possess a talent? And that you have mastered this ability to the extent that you can present yourself as the best at it? Now is the moment to establish a company based on your unique skill.

Being number one in your expertise doesn't guarantee that your business will generate a profit once established. This is yet another pitfall that novice entrepreneurs often fall victim to.

When most people start a business, they anticipate a fast start. They cannot wait to begin reinvesting their riches. However, this occurrence is uncommon; when it doesn't, most people lose interest and move on to other things.

You must learn to be patient to correct this portion of the calculation. I can tell you from personal experience that this phase of the path to financial independence may be even more difficult than when you were working menial jobs to produce income.

In part three of this method, you will rely on a mixture of all the principles you learned in parts one and two to help you survive the winter season.

You will be required to acquire new skills, such as advertising your products and services, running a successful business, managing people and material resources, and attracting and retaining lifelong customers.

Your ability to learn and thrive in these areas will determine your firm's success. Still, suppose you persevere and implement all you've learned without discounting integrity and ethical behavior in your organization. In that case, you will reach a point where the profit you believed would not materialize or arrive too late will be the norm.

When you reach that point, you will need to apply everything you have learned in steps 1, 2, and 3, but this time, you will do it better, faster, and more efficiently, and as you continue to do so, you will continue to expand. That is my foolproof strategy for generating wealth.

PART 5 - INVEST IN SELF.

Believe the greatest investment you can ever make is in yourself; this is self-investment. Financial education is the key to achieving your goals. Investing in your financial education is prudent, as this divides the poor from the wealthy, whether you like it or not.

I included financial education because it is essential, but there are innumerable other ways to invest in yourself. You can invest money to obtain a higher degree in your field of expertise, which would elevate you beyond your contemporaries.

For instance, if you spend $1,000 on a professional course that, upon completion, boosts your marketability and increases your annual income from, say, $100,000 to $300,000, isn't that a sensible investment?

The advantage of this type of investment is that it rarely fails. Unlike an investment in a restaurant that a future Flood could destroy, you would retain the information for the rest of your life. Unlike investing in the capital market, which could be a bit tricky, this form of investment cannot go wrong.

Almost as if your money has purchased your time. The more one invests in oneself, the less effort is required to earn more money. This explains why some specialists might charge up to $1,000 for a task that may not take more than an hour to complete. In this category are, to name a few, highly compensated plastic surgeons, motivational speakers, professional salespeople, and newscasters.

The reasoning behind this is that you should choose a topic you wish to master, which may or may not be the field you are currently in, and educate yourself to the maximum level so that people start paying you a premium for your services and it can be any sector or job, from being a professional copywriter to a sports analyst; just aim for the top of the career ladder, and you will be on your way to wealth.

In a matter of minutes, life may change from steady and predictable to fast-paced and stressful. As our life evolves, so must we! Whether in your personal or professional life, self-growth and self-improvement are essential for coping with the stress of change and accepting the upcoming natural changes.

Self-development involves being honest with oneself and considering what one's top priorities in life should be. It entails acquiring new skills, knowledge, and methods to help you advance personally and professionally.

When you invest in personal development and self-improvement, you also invest in your future and obtain the self-assurance and inner strength necessary to reach success and fulfillment.

Of course, priorities change as time marches on, so assessing your goals and priorities frequently will assist in creating a clear picture of where you wish to be and how you can use your strengths to your greatest advantage. Here are five recommendations to help you understand yourself better and live your life to the fullest.

Positivity!

A good attitude and outlook are essential for personal development and growth. Positive and negative experiences are a part of life, and we must learn from each. For instance, if you attempted to start a small business and failed terribly, you should not be discouraged from trying again. You should use your mistakes in that business to assist you in succeeding in your future endeavor.

Understand the Past.

The previous point leads me to this one. Learn from past decisions to better yourself in the future. If every action we took in life resulted in perfection, we wouldn't learn anything, would we? Indeed, life would be rather dull!

I believe that failure is necessary for success. This does not have to mean utter failure but making mistakes and learning from them is an integral part of a happy life and self-development process.

Each Step in Turn.

Take one goal or endeavor at a time and gain knowledge from it. Yes, multitasking is a terrific talent, but you risk losing interest, concentration, and focus toward the end. The problem with multitasking is that it leads to burnout if you take on too much.

After completing one goal or endeavor, go on to the next. For instance, if you want to learn the power of social media marketing, you should start by joining one social networking site.

Whether it is Facebook, Twitter, or LinkedIn, learning one site first can help you familiarize yourself with the world of social media and develop valuable contacts who can assist you with learning the others when you're ready.

Consider Others.

Sometimes personal development starts with the tale of another's development. Yes, you are reading right! Everyone around us has a story that can benefit us. Consult someone who has opened a small business if you aspire to do so.

This individual will have learned from common mistakes and guide you in the proper route. You will be able to obtain new knowledge and useful guidance that will assist you in being the small business owner you aspire to be.

Accept Change with Wide-Open Arms.

When you change, you grow. It is that easy, and when you can accept and adapt to change, you are well on your path to achieving personal accountability and success.

EXCELLENT METHODS TO INVEST IN YOURSELF.

If money can generate income, can time do the same? You only reach 18, 28, 38, 48, and 58 once. Do you make any personal investments? Please remember that your finest investment is in your future.

Do you take the time to consider your goals?

Do you desire a promotion?

Do you wish to generate many revenue streams?

Do you wish to launch your own company?

Do you wish to become fit?

Do you desire a healthier lifestyle?

Once you know what you want and where you are, determining where you want to be is easier. Now is the time to start drafting your company plan and see it through.

Why now?

Because you cannot afford to take risks, you are not immune to job loss, recession, excessive inflation, or being laid off. Investing in yourself is a terrific approach to having a Plan B if you need to find new ways to pay your bills and maintain your lifestyle. If you don't know how to spend your time, others will probably do so for you.

However, it is not too late; here are six techniques to regain self-investment:

1) Consume better foods and exercise for fitness - Health / Fitness.

The first thing you should invest in is your health and fitness. Without these, you could not do the remaining tasks. Your energy level is mostly determined by how much you exercise and what you consume.

Consume a diet of nutritious and readily available foods for your health. Where else does exercise make you healthier than when your brain releases hormones that make you feel alert and in a good mood?

Your Rewards for Fitness / Health:

- Improved vitality, strength, endurance, health, and physical fitness.
- Feels more confident with a more favorable body image.
- Stay away from diseases and illnesses.

2) Read other books and attend seminars/courses - Knowledge / Abilities.

"Knowledge is power" implies that reading books is not a waste of time; thus, stop watching television and start reading. Reading more books increases your knowledge and expertise.

"Improve your talents" - To remain competitive, you must stay a lifelong learner. Force yourself to read one book per month. Invest in yourself by enrolling in courses to study a second language, pursuing a master's degree or professional certification, or joining a seminar or class for like-minded people.

Your Compensation for Knowledge / Abilities:

- Improve your creativity and produce other ideas for further rewards.
- Explore and rediscover your capability about your requirements and desires.
- Confident and competitive in other aspects of life, you can be able to do more than you now do.

3) To feel nice, perform more acts of generosity and meditation - Morals / Emotions.

If you believe that the more you give, the more you will receive, lend a hand to someone needing financial or professional assistance. I am confident you will feel fantastic and receive more than you offer.

You are not only feeling fantastic, but you are also making a friend for life. Have you considered meditating for 10 minutes per day? If you are feeling emotionally disturbed or stressed out. Meditation is a tried-and-true way of calming the mind; you will see things more clearly after a session.

Your Benefits for Ethics / Emotions:

- Be cheerful most of the time.
- Understand your emotions and keep you focused on your desired goals.
- Cultivate a cheerful attitude and be a soul mate that everyone desires as a friend.

4) Spend time with relatives to maintain your joy - Family / Partner.

While avidly pursuing your goals, you can occasionally feel that something is in your way and feel horrible about it. Negativity can sometimes be overwhelming. You should eliminate all this negativity and charge up positivity by spending time with family, as this eliminates negativity and generates joy.

Your Family / Spouse Rewards:

- Family and husband relationship improvement
- Through improved communication, a family can avoid misunderstandings and feel closer together.

5) Commence personal finance and investment for wealth - Finances / Investment

Get out of debt, start organizing your finances and create a portfolio of investments to put your money to work. Spending a little time each day on your finances will yield enormous returns. In today's society, it may be difficult to sustain solely one source of income; therefore, it is important to produce various income streams from innovative ideas.

Your Investment / Financial Returns:

- Develop budgeting and prudent spending habits.
- Stay out of debt and use your interests to build many income streams.
- Increased financial intelligence leads to financial independence.

6) Networking and obtaining community assistance - Society / Community.

The power of a single intellect is limited; you must find other like-minded individuals for strength and support. Relationships with others can facilitate self-improvement by allowing you to share perspectives and receive advice/support from someone who has been there before, allowing you to avoid common traps and save time. Spending time with friends and strangers will make a significant difference in pursuing your goals.

Your Reward for Contributing to Society / Community:

- Avoid frequent mistakes and obtain essential information you can have missed.
- You can receive emotional support and assistance as needed through mentorship and masterminding.
- Improve your social skills and utilize your friends for support and inspiration.

Investments can make or ruin an individual depending on how well they are made. There are general laws of investing that can be followed to reduce the investor's exposure to risk. These are not foolproof, but they are decent suggestions for protecting your money and investments.

The final investment goal should be one of the initial considerations for investors. A retirement fund is a choice for the long term, although money for a family vacation or other expenses may necessitate a riskier investment such as equities. The retirement fund can be as basic as an IRA, or some CDs were hidden away in a bank for 20 years since the funds will not be required immediately.

Diversification is a term often used by investors and financial consultants for good reason. When it comes to investing, the adage "Don't put all your eggs in one basket" rings quite true. By diversifying their investments, the investor can protect their entire net worth if one or more investments fail.

For instance, a person who invests solely in stocks relies greatly on the market, not just maintaining stability and rising but also never dropping. The astute investor selects different CDs, equities, retirement accounts, and mutual funds to attain this equilibrium. This helps to protect them if one of their investments fails.

Maintain a goal perspective; do not depart from your financial strategy out of emotion. By reacting rashly when a news brief throws you a curveball or the market declines marginally for the day, you can toss away a long-term investment that would have been beneficial.

Focus on the long-term goal and adhere to purchasing or selling investments when they reach a specified value rather than basing your decisions on daily trends or scars.

One of the most fundamental rules of investing is considering the impact of taxes and inflation on the overall bottom line. Taxes creep up on an investor because they are not a large number at once, such as a market decline, and if not closely monitored, they can put a significant hole in any investments.

Ensure that the profits generated are sufficient to pay taxes and inflation and reach your investment goal.

PART 6 – DIVERSIFIED.

Diversification is a "clever" term used by certain financial advisors when attempting to sell you on a company's shares or their strategy of outperforming the market. It is indicative of either or both arrogance or avarice.

Diversification is a proven approach for mitigating investment risk. Modern Portfolio Theory and the work of Harry Markowitz are the sources of this concept. It is common sense that if your wealth is concentrated in a small number of investments, you face greater risk than someone with wealth dispersed over many investments.

The typical response is, "This company is the best since Thomas Edison created General Electric." It will exceed Wal-Mart, Microsoft and IBM combined.

Perhaps but you can't predict the future. Regardless of how promising a company's future may appear, there is always a risk.

- The product you believe would be successful fails in the marketplace.

- The founder had a heart attack and died.

- An act of terrorism destroys the company's global headquarters.

- The vice president of marketing may have sold controlled narcotics.

- A government agency concludes that the corporation violated the law.

- The company is subject to a massive class action lawsuit.

- The central American government seizes the company's principal manufacturing facility.

Possibilities are infinite. Regardless of how promising a company's long-term prospects may appear, it's virtually inevitable that it will encounter some difficulty. You will not truly know if it's the next Wal-Mart or McDonald's until you see whether or not it solves those difficulties. And so forth.

Non-systemic or idiosyncratic risk is the risk associated with investing in a single company and relying on its survival and growth despite its challenges.

With the introduction of the vehicle, all horse buggy enterprises failed, regardless of management quality. Consequently, the logical option is to invest in two businesses. If one fails, the other will likely succeed. However, there is still a substantial possibility that both businesses may fail. This is especially true if their industries are similar.

Therefore, investing in different companies in diverse areas is the logical solution.

Modern portfolio theory has found that investing in twenty companies in diverse industries minimizes approximately 90 percent of the non-systemic risk. Investing in thirty companies eliminates any systemic risk.

This means that your only risk is what is known as "market risk" — the possibility that all 30 companies decline due to macroeconomic variables such as high-interest rates or a global downturn.

However, the flip side of reducing non-market risk is eliminating non-market GAIN. Thus, when you have thirty or more stocks, you won't lose more than the market as a whole, but neither will your portfolio gain more than the market.

A handful of your thirty stocks will increase significantly, most will perform on average, and a few will decline. Therefore, the average will be relatively similar to the market.

Consider actively managed mutual funds now. Most of them have stock in thirty or more companies.

Most do not outperform the market. They do not retain the stocks they select. They sell some, requiring you to pay taxes on the winners and purchase some, incurring transaction fees.

Not to mention that you pay for your fund manager's salary and other administrative charges, which may be inexpensive (Vanguard, for instance) or costly (most mutual fund families).

The obvious conclusion is that you have a choice between eliminating non-systemic risk by buying and holding a basket of 30 or so stocks in your brokerage account (NOT a mutual fund, where active management will cost you transaction and management fees, plus capital gains taxes) or taking the risk of choosing a few companies you're confident will soar and crossing your fingers.

(One simple strategy to outperform the market is to invest in an index mutual fund, such as Vanguard's S & P 500 index fund. Thus, you will be assured that you will equal the market — which is superior to 90% of actively managed mutual funds.)

Stock analysts dislike this.

This includes mutual fund managers, portfolio managers, brokers, newsletter writers, and financial analysts attempting to offer you their services of predicting which companies will do well.

They enjoy looking for companies that appear to be heading for success, and they often find them. If you invest your entire portfolio in a single firm and it quickly doubles or triples in value, you have outperformed the market

However, if all your investment money is invested in one or a small number of enterprises, you are exposed to this non-systemic risk. If the company doesn't achieve the results predicted by the advisor, your portfolio plummets.

But certainly, there are legitimate reasons why some companies succeed, and others fail, and if you can isolate these causes, you can purchase the stocks that are most likely to succeed and avoid those that are most likely to fail.

This has been the topic of extensive research, and there are markers you can use to identify companies that are more likely to be successful investments.

The prices of all equities in the market can fall precipitously, as they did in 1929. Therefore, you should diversify across asset classes, commonly known as asset allocation. Everyone should ideally own some equities, some cash (money markets or certificates of deposit), some real estate (other than their primary residence), and bonds.

In an ideal world, you should not just own investments in your home nation but also stocks, cash, real estate, and bonds on each continent (excluding Antarctica, for now!). This broadens your exposure across national and regional economies and currencies.

Therefore, whenever you hear someone deride diversification by calling it "diversification" (how cute!), I'd wager (not all of my money but some) that they're a broker or other advisor attempting to sell you a specific company or an advisor trying to sell you their method for selecting winning stocks.

WHY IS DIVERSIFICATION IMPORTANT FOR YOUR PORTFOLIO?

A prudent investor would regularly assess his portfolio's investments. Given the volatile nature of markets, it is essential to diversify one's investments, especially in equities, as putting all of one's money into a single stock would be highly risky.

Eggs in this context refer to stocks, and if an investor invests all of his eggs in the same basket (industry/sector), he would be taking a significant risk. He could suffer significant losses if the chosen industry crashes. The expression "Don't Put All Eggs in One Basket" is likely derived from this experience.

I would also like to illustrate this with a recent example from India. Due to different circumstances, the aviation industry experienced significant churn and volatility in 2016, which had a domino effect on airline stocks.

If a significant portion of an investor's portfolio comprises airline equities, he would have a difficult time as the industry-wide volatility would have caused share prices to plummet substantially.

If the investor had been a little more astute and taken clues from what was happening to his stocks and reevaluated the stock composition of his portfolio, he would have been able to make adjustments before incurring other losses.

Diversifying one's portfolio reduces the risk of loss, particularly when share values change due to market volatility in a specific industry. Ideally, the investor would invest in a wide range of companies from some industries and make additions and subtractions of stocks after periodically analyzing them.

Therefore, in the preceding example, if the investor had distributed his risk over other businesses rather than focusing on the aviation sector, he would have likely gained or suffered much smaller losses.

Countless investors have committed the same mistake as the one described above, namely, investing extensively in a single company or stock with the expectation that it will perform exceptionally well in the short or long term. If an investor has limited knowledge of diversifying their portfolio, it would be smart to seek the counsel of a financial planner.

A financial planner from a reputable source of financial services will be able to comprehend your current investments better and create a practical road map for achieving your financial goals within a specific time frame.

Also, a financial planner with training in financial advisory will be able to provide you with more investment fund possibilities. Historically, only high-net-worth individuals (HNIs) and ultra-high-net-worth individuals (super HNIs) could afford the services of a financial planner.

However, in the last five years, investors have realized that the fees charged by the right financial advisor are negligible if he can guide them in sharpening their portfolio toward their financial goals.

Diversifying a portfolio is necessary for wealth building; therefore, if your portfolio consists primarily of stocks from a single firm or industry, you should diversify it for your benefit.

Diversification of holdings and the Novice Investor.

It is advisable to make important choices and choose a well-diversified portfolio, even if the portfolio is quite small. It would be foolish to try to convey the complete art of portfolio management (especially considering markets change instantaneously and even the most senior portfolio managers still fail to beat them).

A second reason why this argument is irrelevant is that there are no rules and no "certain" decisions when trying to beat the markets. However, supports are available to help investors maintain their equilibrium during turbulent times. Diversification is the most fundamental and, probably, the most essential notion of maintaining a good portfolio, which is the main focus of this section.

Diversification is lowering risk by holding a diverse portfolio of securities. Two types of portfolio risk exist: systematic risk, regardless of how well you diversify, and unsystematic risk, which diversification can avoid.

This section's primary focus will be on the risk that a diversified portfolio of assets can mitigate. This phenomenon is associated with the relationship between securities, quantified by the correlation coefficient. This may sound frightening, but it is merely the movement of stocks inside a portfolio relative to one another.

For instance, if a portfolio consists of two companies and one improves by 10 points while the other decreases by 10 points, these two stocks are said to be negatively connected or correlate -1. If their tendencies are identical and they move 10 points in tandem, the two securities are said to be positively correlated or have a +1 correlation.

Using this approach as a foundation, consider an investor who has invested equally in two General Motors and Ford stocks. Since both General Motors and Ford are US automakers, there is a significant possibility that if one stock declines, the other will shortly follow.

As one might expect, if automobile sales decline, more people will start using public transportation, generating revenue for the bus sector. This is an example of positively correlated assets; as can be seen, holding both companies are quite dangerous. Investing half in Ford and the remainder in a bus firm would be wiser.

This example of a negative correlation demonstrates how diversifying a portfolio's holdings can lessen its total risk. If the bus company's stock and Ford's stock are negatively connected, then the loss of one will be offset by the rise of the other.

One could wonder why the portfolio can only break even if both securities cancel each other out. This would be the case if investments were negatively linked; however, the likelihood of securities moving in tandem is quite low in practice.

Thus, diversification will be advantageous if the correlation between the investments is between 0 and -1. Diversification benefits are more likely to be gotten as long as your portfolio investments don't tend to move together historically or in the prospectus.

There are many instances in history in which this principle was regrettably disregarded. Still, first, one must ask, "Where is my retirement money?" and "In what other investments is my retirement money?"

The significance of these issues stems from the fact that in the late 1990s, a business by the name of Enron experienced some financial difficulties, forcing thousands to lose their investments. The losses were severe but manageable for those with the good fortune to diversify.

Those who held Enron securities exclusively and relied heavily on them for retirement lost everything. Investing solely in the company for which the investor works is a common mistake made by inexperienced investors, who fail to recognize that they are also portfolio managers and must actively hedge their risk.

Diversification should be considered for all sorts of securities, not just stocks. Maintaining a balanced portfolio of real estate, bonds, small and large stocks, and Treasury bills can make the difference between large losses and spectacular gains.

Studies indicate that professional fund managers are no better at outperforming the market than the typical investor, despite decades of efforts to achieve a constant return above the market. This provides even more justification for holding a diverse portfolio.

When investors purchase a stock, they are unaware of its price 24 hours later. Hopefully, he or she researched the investment to ensure it was a good buy, but it is impossible to predict where the investment will close the next day.

Using diversification as support, inexperienced security managers may reduce most of the risk connected with these unforeseen changes, decreasing the impact of our losses and assisting us in becoming more successful investors.

THE SIGNIFICANCE OF DIVERSIFICATION FOR WEALTH CREATION.

You have probably heard the expression, "don't put all your eggs in one basket." When it comes to investments, you don't place all your eggs in one basket. This chapter will examine the various investing "baskets" and outline our diversification strategy.

Everyone has a fear of financial loss. We do not wish to make financial choices that result in capital loss. Diversification reduces the likelihood of this happening.

Some investments have the potential to generate greater profits, but they also carry more short-term risks. Other investments generate returns that are lower but more stable.

Diversification is intended to provide smoother and more consistent investment returns over time.

1: Invest following your time horizon.

When we meet with you, we spend considerable time learning about your aims and goals. Any investment strategy we offer must suit you and provide you with every opportunity to accomplish your needs and goals.

If you have short-term financial goals (less than three years), we recommend cash investments such as bank accounts and term deposits. Although these investments may not generate substantial returns, your capital will remain stable.

If your goals are more long-term, you can incorporate investments, such as stocks and real estate, that have the potential to provide higher returns over time. You would not invest in stocks for one year since it is too hazardous. In contrast, putting all your money in cash for a decade is similarly dangerous, as it would hardly keep up with inflation after taxes are deducted.

Depending on your time horizon, you could invest some of your funds in growth assets for higher returns.

2 - Various eggs in different baskets.

Having all your money invested in a single property or stock is dangerous. You could earn substantial returns if it performs well, but what if it fails?

Good diversification entails investing in different asset classes, including stocks, real estate, fixed-income securities, and cash. How much you invest in each sector relies on your goals and goals and the level of risk you're willing to accept to reach your desired return.

Over time, you will see that different asset classes do well at various times of the year.

3: Take from the good and give to the evil.

We feel that rebalancing your portfolio is essential.

Consider the recommendation that you invest approximately 30 percent of your portfolio in Australian shares. Approximately 35% of your portfolio comprises Australian shares, expected to generate exceptional returns over the coming year. If Australian shares account for 5% more of your portfolio than before, other sectors will be under-allocated.

This is not easy to accomplish when things are going well. Possibly, if Australian shares perform the following year strongly, you will regret selling down last year. However, if the value of that sector decreases, you will appreciate the advice we provided and your discipline in adhering to the recommended asset allocation.

In contrast, when Australian shares have a difficult year and decrease, we will recommend transferring funds from sectors that have performed better to Australian shares.

4 - Use diverse investment models.

Superannuation is the most suitable financial instrument for many individuals when saving for retirement. However, the further you are from retirement, the greater the likelihood that the super rules will change.

Perhaps the change will not be significant, but we believe it is hazardous to make significant decisions based on the premise that today's laws will still apply when you retire in 10 years.

We propose you diversify across multiple investment vehicles. We favor superannuation as the primary vehicle for retirement savings but would also recommend managed funds and bank accounts.

If the rules change, you have not placed all your eggs in one basket.

5 - Don't concentrate on a single investment.

Concentrating your wealth accumulation on a single investment is risky. I have seen people with a single investment property and a substantial mortgage struggle when they can't find tenants for six months.

I have had clients with big shareholdings in a single firm (through an employee share scheme) experience a 40% reduction in wealth over a few weeks owing to the decline in that company's share price.

So, distribute your eggs.

Suppose you have money invested in five different stocks. If one of these businesses fails, you will lose 20% of your cash. What if it was invested in one hundred companies, one of which failed? You would lose only 1% of your capital.

6: Don't forget the pencils.

As a last illustration of the significance of diversification, consider this case.

Imagine you are holding a pencil made of lead. It is feasible to bend and break it, although it may need some effort.

Now, gather and collect twenty pencils in your hands. Try to bend and break them, but you cannot.

ARE YOU DIVERSIFYING YOUR INVESTMENTS SUFFICIENTLY?

The premise behind this advice is that if you invest in multiple types of assets and one decline, the others may rise, resulting in a more stable or less volatile return over time.

The underlying premise is that the investments you purchase are distinct and will offset each other in all market conditions. Most literature discusses stocks, bonds, and possibly real estate as investments, but does this encompass all viable avenues of accumulating wealth?

What challenges does this strategy present?

4) Diversification in the conventional sense is effective 99.9% of the time but that 1% is becoming increasingly prevalent, and standard loss prevention strategies may no longer be effective.

Diversification is contingent on 1) the balance between buy and sell orders, 2) the degree of interconnectedness within the markets in question, and 3) the systematic factor of issuing money in conjunction with leverage, which may trump the ability of the buyer and seller (or the market) to agree on prices.

1. A buyer or seller will always be available to complete a transaction in a balanced market.

You would need to cut the price of the investment you are selling if no one is interested, but the transaction would still be completed at a steady price. If nobody wants it, you cannot sell it and complete the transaction; therefore, your investment will be worthless.

This phenomenon occurs when a market crashes - everyone wants to sell their positions simultaneously, and no one buys, causing prices to drop quickly. In this instance, the market would be unbalanced, and diversification would only lower volatility in markets that are not unbalanced.

2. Interconnectedness is the degree to which marketplaces are interconnected.

This concept can be comprehended starting with the local investment climate. If you purchase Canadian bonds, they will all be affected by the same variables, including Canadian interest rates, political environment, economy, and regulations.

Some factors affect Canadian equities and bonds but not in the same way. For instance, increased interest rates directly impact bond prices due to the law of compounding and the rule of arbitrage (the markets will adjust the price of something until all the possible instruments carry the same or an equivalent price).

Buying Canadian and American stocks and bonds will further reduce the number of common elements. As more worldwide investments are purchased, there is less common ground, as certain economies will prosper, and others will decline.

The economic cycle, interest rate, currencies, consumer spending patterns, trade, and regulation in each country will be so dissimilar that investments will typically move in opposing directions. Diversification is effective due to variances in the market climates.

What would happen if all economies were interconnected?

What if all the world's interest rates were interconnected?

What if all economies experienced simultaneous expansion and contraction? Diversification:

Would it make a difference?

All the stocks you own would function as a single unit. If all underlying drivers moved in unison, the global bond market would respond identically. If there were a scenario where individuals sold everything out of fear, everything would decline simultaneously.

Is there any interconnectedness?

How did the 2011 Eurozone crisis affect our portfolios in Canada?

Affected by this crisis were China, Japan, Brazil, and Russia.

What about the Icelandic bond market or an Irish bank? All these events had an impact on our investments.

How? Due to technology, the coupling of the world's economies through trade agreements, the global sharing of labor through outsourcing, globally uniform commodity pricing, and derivatives that may be sold anywhere and have an impact, the world's economies are interdependent.

Since derivatives can be linked to any investment, counterparty risk or the risk that the parties involved will not pay for their wagers plays a significant role in connecting markets.

If, for example, a healthy European bank invests in bad American mortgages, it will be harmed in the same way as American banks, even though the European bank's operations have not changed. Does the year 2008 ring any bells of recognition? So, what can diversification accomplish if the global economy is a single massive entity?

Diversification is beneficial in a "normal market" where buying and selling forces are balanced, and prices do not fluctuate excessively. When selling, you might obtain a constant price.

The same will occur if you wish to purchase. There would be sufficient disagreements for the market to work. This will not be the case if everyone is afraid and the market is imbalanced.

3. The third assumption is the combination of money issuance and leverage.

If there were one million shares of a small mining business, each worth $2, the total value of the shares traded would be $2 million.

What would occur if an individual with $10 million began purchasing shares to spend the entire sum?

The price of shares would increase. Not only that, but if every shareholder sold their shares to this individual, he would be able to set the price by himself.

If he desired to pay $5 per share, the price of the shares would be $5 per share. If he chose $10 per share, the cost would be $10. Assume that just a small proportion of the initial stockholders sold their shares. If 100,000 shares were sold at $10 each, just $1 million would be expended.

This individual has $9 million left to spend. If the original stockholders were to hold on for other price hikes, the remaining $9 million could continue to drive up prices. Since "much money is pursuing a set number of shares," the initial $1 per share price can be multiplied by a significant amount.

Notice that no other factors, such as the industry, the economy, the company's fundamentals, management, or regulations, are considered in determining the stock price - not even technical indications such as price history or price-volume indicators.

The price rises because a large amount of money is purchasing shares. This is how pump-and-dump scams operate. No aggressive selling technique is used to induce individuals to buy shares, and there is no rapid withdrawal of speculators' funds that triggers the ensuing crash.

What is the purpose of this narrative?

A similar pattern emerges when examining the entire stock market and the origins of capital. The Federal Reserve and European Central Bank are "printing money" or issuing significant new debt. All the newly issued debt must enter the financial system; otherwise, it will not be issued. What will happen to stock prices if $1 trillion is printed and placed on the stock market?

Because this amount of money is so huge, it will overshadow all other indicators and cause prices to rise because so much money is pursuing stocks. This applies to all markets, including bonds, commodities, and derivatives, and it would also work in reverse if equivalent quantities of money were withdrawn from a market.

When these central banks issue money, it is multiplied by a factor of many, so the impact is considerably bigger than the numbers show. As an illustration, if $1 trillion of new money was released as new debt, leverage might generate $10 trillion in new derivatives contracts.

As of June 2011, the derivatives industry is expected to be worth $700 TRILLION. In comparison, the world equity market was approximately $50 trillion in April 2011, the bond market was over $90 trillion in December 2010, and the world gross domestic product was $60 trillion.

If you recall the previous stock tale, the quote was, "a lot of money is pursuing a set number of shares." These two situations are comparable because the underlying phenomenon is identical. This means derivatives can significantly impact other markets and influence the direction of prices, just as in the preceding stock example.

Solutions:

Given this situation, what should a person do? Traditional methods of diversification should continue to be utilized but should be expanded. Most investors initially purchased bonds, followed by Canadian stocks, US stocks, worldwide stocks, global debt, commodities, and derivatives.

It is optimal to purchase a combination of these assets that do not have a strong correlation or don't react similarly to market happenings. If these tools are interconnected, where might you diversify next?

The key to maximizing the benefits of diversification in the past was continually expanding your opportunity set to include increasingly unusual investments. Ironically, the way to diversify further is to return to fundamentals.

Why? The fundamentals are not as interdependent as typical investments; if anything catastrophic occurs, the fundamentals will always be sought after or consumed.

What are fundamentals?

Cash on hand would be the first one. It does not rise or fall with market fluctuations until significant inflation or the currency's value is changed through devaluation or another modification.

Holding cash also allows you to purchase an item at a reduced price, which decreases your risk compared to purchasing it at a higher price. Gold and silver are the world's currencies. Thus, the next notion is owning various types of cash. In the past, these were used as currency, and this could occur again in the future.

These can be invested in via gold shares and real metal. If you have the knowledge and resources, it may be worthwhile to consider purchasing land for many purposes, such as renting, energy generating, food production, or future development.

The following inquiry is, "what does money buy?" why do I require it? If you obtain items immediately, you do not require cash. This is where bartering and self-production can be considered. This concept is extended via communal barter, cash, and localizing production whenever possible. This is creating items directly as a team, as opposed to individually.

Once it complies with the norms of trade - it stores value, it is consistent, conveniently available, standardized and everyone who uses it believes it to be valuable - anything can be used as a currency. Launching a firm and establishing a trading network could be an extension of this concept.

The future of diversification will be founded on innovation and an economy that allows people to succeed via innovation. Diversification is a wonderful notion, but it should be expanded to guarantee that it is effective in as feasible as possible.

INVESTMENT PRUDENCE THROUGH PORTFOLIO DIVERSIFICATION.

Diversification is if there is one timeless investment principle that tops all others, among the very best. If you ask one hundred random people on the street to define diversification, you will likely receive 100 unique responses. To ensure everybody is on the same page, it is essential to establish clear definitions at the outset.

Diversification is not about achieving "higher returns," as is a frequent misunderstanding. Diversification is primarily concerned with limiting risk, not with maximizing rewards. The two are not mutually exclusive, but it goes to reason that you have a greater chance of earning a bigger return on investment if you are ready to assume greater risk.

Diversification is a vital fundamental money management approach that must be performed to attain your long-term financial goals while limiting risk, even though it does not guarantee against loss.

Suppose you examine the investment patterns of families and their wealth that has persisted over many generations. In that case, you will realize that diversification has a much deeper meaning for people who wish to succeed in every conceivable economic and political environment.

The goal of this section is to discuss the most essential factors of achieving true portfolio diversification.

The term "portfolio" typically refers to an individual's collection of investments. Your portfolio covers your entire life, and we tend to overlook that it is more than just a reflection of what we put directly into retirement assets.

To better understand your portfolio, it may be helpful to see it as a representation of your net worth. Looking at your portfolio from that perspective allows you to choose which assets may be under or over-allocated so you can plan accordingly.

Knowledge and expertise are the most precious things you can possess, and one thing I have observed over the years is that too many people buy into the dream of passive income without understanding the process.

Developing many streams of passive income does not occur quickly. Although we may be focused on expanding our wealth in a hands-off, passive manner, it still takes an initiative-taking attitude and a solid money management technique.

"Never put all eggs in one basket" - You've heard this sensible adage repeatedly throughout your life. However, this golden rule of investing is often abused and misinterpreted.

Even while the concept of having a well-diversified "basket" of investments in many financial asset classes and businesses to limit risk exposure sounds intuitive, many investors do not adhere to it correctly.

Some investors do not get what it means to have a diversified portfolio, while others ignore it.

As you are about to discover, there's more to diversification than selecting a few "set and forget" investment vehicles, depositing funds, and handing over control to someone else.

Market diversification, asset allocation, and risk management comprise the pillars of successful long-term investing.

As any financial advisor or someone with a modicum of common sense will tell you, the best strategy to safeguard your portfolio is to spread your risk capital across many asset classes and investment kinds.

Thus, you can reduce the likelihood of a single investment or asset class destroying the overall performance of your portfolio.

These asset types typically consist of different stocks, bonds, certificates of deposit, and mutual funds.

Frankly, I cringe whenever I hear well-meaning investors - the ones who've only played it safe their entire lives - suggest that everyone should "hedge" against a stock market crash, terrorist attack, or natural disaster by loading up their retirement portfolios with low-yielding bank CDs or Treasury notes that lock up their money for 5 to 10 years.

Not only will these investments leave you barely treading water to keep up with inflation (the invisible tax), but when the bulk of your investment portfolio consists of strongly correlated asset classes, your overall risk might climb dramatically.

Investment Methodology.

Many people have ambitions. They just lack the plan to reach their goals. A proverb states, "If you fail to plan, you plan to fail."

While most reasonable individuals would not travel to an unfamiliar location without a road map or directions, far too many investors attempt to navigate the financial world without an investment road map.

Before investing any money, you must have distinct goals and a plan for achieving them. Here, your risk aversion and investment strategy come into play.

But there is a caveat: With so many various sorts of individual investments to pick from, things can rapidly become very confusing, especially if you have not done your research or do not know where to start.

Like wolves in a hen house, traditional investing firms utilize "convenience" as their main selling point to get you to invest your hard-earned money with them and leave it in their hands until your financial goals are reached or until you retire (if that happens to be your aim) (if that happens to be your goal).

But this strategy of expanding your nest fund is simply too dangerous. It makes more sense to adopt an investment strategy that increases your current income and allows you to recoup your principle much sooner instead of waiting until you are too old to enjoy it (or never get to enjoy it at all).

A professional advisor can ensure that you are not investing more than you should (or less than you should) and assist you in calculating and establishing what must occur for you to achieve your financial goals.

Whether or not you opt to employ the services of a licensed expert is secondary to your ability to answer key questions regarding your family's financial stability with candor.

What goals do you expect to accomplish with your investments?

Will you be covering the cost of college? Purchasing a home? Retiring soon?

Do you possess the intestinal fortitude (guts) to withstand the roller coaster ride and potential losses connected with high-risk investments?

Do you have sufficient time before retirement and sufficient savings to rely on passive investment returns, or do you need higher returns to reach your retirement goals?

These are just a few examples of the types of questions you must be able to answer to maximize the benefits of diversification.

Investing is comparable to a game in which the winner is unknown until after the game has been completed. Whenever you play a game, there is typically a method you can employ to maximize your chances of winning; investing is no exception.

Investing works best when you keep it simple. People tend to overcomplicate every aspect of investing, so making it more difficult than it is.

Investing successfully is comparable to gardening, not winning the lottery. You must plant many seeds because the birds will consume part of them.

Some will flourish while others wither, and constant weeding will always be necessary (and the occasional pests to deal with).

But if you handle things properly (and keep your "greed monster"), your investments have the best chance of continuing to grow.

You can gently nudge them, but rapid development is typically unsteady and fragile and can fall on you. You will eventually have some "money trees" that have grown to the point where they generate a substantial passive income.

Wealth results from how hard you work, how much you make, how much your money earns, and the length of time that your money compounds.

Regardless of your long-term goals, producing a continuous passive income is not always simple, but as long as you know what you want, have a plan, and stick to it, nothing can prevent you from accomplishing your financial goals.

Suppose you are currently enjoying the higher stages of life. Congratulations! I have discovered that the trip is more enjoyable than the destination.

EXIT TECHNIQUES AND DIVERSIFICATION.

In these difficult circumstances, revisiting some fundamental fundamentals of wealth management and protection is important. There are many reasons to reevaluate how your firm is positioned related to your exit plans in light of the current economic climate.

It has been said, "To get rich, you must own many things but to stay rich, you must own different diverse things."

Therefore, the question becomes, "Do you currently hold too much of a single asset - your privately owned firm - which could compromise your total wealth preservation strategy?"

This is the question you should ask yourself:

Am I seeking to continue "becoming rich" or to "remain affluent?"

If you wish to "remain wealthy," you need an exit strategy plan to protect your illiquid corporate riches. You will likely wish to monetize a portion (or the entirety) of your business interest to DIVERSIFY your wealth.

Another excellent inquiry to ask yourself is:

"Would I invest all the profits from the sale of my firm today in a single stock that doesn't have an actively traded market?"

The answer is probably a resounding "NO" because the RISK of owning only one stock at this time in your life is too great. This financial plan has a single point of failure since the investment is NOT DIVERSIFIED.

This is the current financial reality for many privately held business owners.

Most of your wealth is "tied up" in your privately held company.

If this is the case, it would be prudent to ask, "Why am I not more DIVERSIFIED?"

Often, a business owner will respond in one of the following ways:

"I don't view my business as a RISK" or "I am not ready to SELL the business. Therefore, I can't DIVERSIFY."

"I am not ready to SELL the business; therefore, I can't DIVERSIFY," or "If I had to sell my business in order to diversify my wealth, I would not be able to do it at this time."

To protect my loved ones financially in the case of my untimely demise, I have taken out a sizeable life insurance policy (i.e., "my mortality is the only RISK that I truly consider to exist affecting the future success of my firm").

My business sells various products and/or services; I am DIVERSIFIED.

You can be willing to acknowledge, "I have not yet committed to learning about exit strategy planning to safeguard my riches properly."

Many business owners have not yet committed to learning about exit strategy planning. Still, they would prefer to safeguard their capital against difficult economic times like the one we are currently experiencing. However, an exit strategy plan aligns with your goals to allow you to quit your firm in the manner and timeframe you deem most suitable.

Therefore, the issue becomes, "What must occur for you to start considering Exit Strategies?"

Examine WHY it is challenging for a successful business owner to concentrate on an Exit Strategy.

As the proprietor of a firm, you are the master of your fate. You have overcome the odds against "making it" in business and continue to do so daily. Considering an exit strategy plan typically "goes against the grain" of thoughts of business growth and expansion.

How can you start transforming this Titanic way of thinking into an exit strategy plan that safeguards all your earned wealth?

Well, the only logical response to this question is to seek the advice of people who have already exited their businesses and to gather the knowledge you need to "think thoughts" about leaving your firm.

The gathering of information on exit strategy preparation prompts thoughts of leaving the firm.

Most of the time, thoughts of leaving your firm are accompanied by sensations of 'time and financial independence.'

And if these exit-related thoughts and emotions persist for a sufficient period, you will secure your money with a well-timed and well-thought-out exit strategy plan.

Then, you will judge your success in part based on how diverse your exit strategy plan has made you.

In conclusion, most business owners will decide when they are fully prepared. Therefore, we can only continue to emphasize to the millions of business owners out there that diversification is essential to securing the success you have spent a lifetime achieving.

In this light, one may argue that it is never too early to consider an exit strategy, and we leave you with the warning that the only method for a good Exit Strategy is a proactive one.

DIVERSIFICATION IS THE KEY TO INDIVIDUAL WEALTH.

It takes time and effort to amass riches; very few of the worlds affluent were born wealthy; the vast majority earned their fortunes through hard work.

Ask anyone who has more money in the bank than the typical worker, and they will tell you that they worked extremely hard in the past and continue to do so to maintain their fortunes. They will also tell you that diversifying as much as you can afford is one of the finest methods to convert your investment into riches.

Most of us are on a tight budget when we first start, and we look for short-term financial gains that will fill our bank accounts. However, unless you win the lottery, this is unlikely to occur. It takes time and effort to build riches and sufficient financial stability to sustain it.

Any member of the millionaire or billionaire club will emphasize diversification of investments, analogous to not placing all your eggs in one basket. There are so many options to invest your money in that it may be difficult to decide which ones to pursue. Before investing, observe the tendencies of the various markets for some time.

Opening a 401(k) and investing through a mutual fund is a smart place to start; this is a relatively safe way to invest, and the long-term returns can be satisfactory. Once you begin to see earnings in your mutual fund, you can want to try investing a portion of your profits in other markets.

Investing in the Forex money market is a good approach to achieving bigger gains in a shorter period, but you must grasp how this market operates to make a profit. Find a credible provider whose software provides a training program and study it well before investing.

Purchasing government treasury bonds and bills is a fairly secure investment; depending on which you purchase, the yield can be quite high. The one redeeming quality is that these bonds are backed by the US government, which is unlikely to declare bankruptcy, so your money is assured to be safe.

Take your time and invest intelligently; you will have a financially secure future. The more diversified your portfolio, the more money you can earn to create wealth.

Try what I did if you need money immediately or within the hour. I am making more money today than I did in my previous business, and you can, too, if you click the link below and read the incredible true tale. I was suspicious for only ten seconds after joining before I knew what this was. You will also be beaming from ear to ear, as I was.

Imagine tripling your money each week with negligible or no risk! To locate a list of verified Million Dollar Corporations giving 75% commission on their products.

After deciding to retire, many individuals are most concerned about running out of money. Diversifying retirement income sources helps to lessen this risk. Diversification is one of the most valuable components of a financial plan since it can lower the chance of running out of money.

Most retirees have various sources of income to support their lifestyles. Social Security benefits are available starting at age 62. Accounts for retirement and private savings can be invested in multiple asset classes. Insurance firms provide fixed annuities that can generate a steady monthly income.

Social Security and fixed annuity payments are guaranteed but may not be sufficient to meet all costs. Each of these sources of income carries risks. Therefore, none is ideal.

Also, they may not keep pace with inflation, jeopardizing the capacity to sustain purchasing power over time if they are the sole source of income. Guarantees for fixed annuities are contingent on the ability of the issuing insurance company to pay claims.

Investing in stocks and bonds is another option to consider while seeking retirement income. Stocks offer greater potential for capital appreciation but are riskier and may drop in value. Generally speaking, bonds offer higher interest rates than fixed annuities.

Bonds bear the same risk of value decline as equities until they reach maturity. Neither stocks nor bonds provide monthly cash flow. Most bonds will pay interest biannually. Quarterly dividends may or may not be paid on stocks. However, many pay no dividends at all.

Diversification helps mitigate the risk associated with relying just on one source of retirement income. Social Security and a fixed annuity payment might provide a monthly income base as part of a comprehensive approach. Investments in retirement accounts and other savings can be utilized to supplement fixed payments and generate long-term growth.

A diverse portfolio can protect against unforeseeable catastrophes. Many retirees are concerned that they may outlive their funds. Fixed annuities can alleviate this issue depending on the payment option you select. Thus, a fixed annuity can function as long-term care insurance.

Social Security and fixed annuities may be useful for providing a stable income, but they don't meet lump sum demands. Those who preserve a portion of their wealth in liquid investments such as stocks and bonds can use them to meet huge emergency bills if necessary. A second concern is that a significant expense, such as a hefty medical bill, will occur early in retirement.

Not only does diversification, the second golden rule of successful investing, entail never putting too many eggs in a basket that must also be appropriately balanced between fixed income and equities, but the all-important equity section of portfolios must also be subdivided into a sufficient number of sub-sectors further to disperse risk across an adequate number of individual stocks.

With Canada constituting only 2% to 3% of the global stock market value, it is imperative to diversify abroad to access more and better investment opportunities. Foreign mutual funds, exchange-traded funds, or U.S. and Canadian firms with substantial worldwide operations might be used to attain global diversification.

In such a search, it will be discovered that there is an abundance of foreign stocks to choose from, with trust in the information sources upon which such decisions are founded being essential.

The necessity for diversification also emphasizes the significance of statistical significance for individual portfolio holdings. In other words, individual assets should not become too little to contribute meaningfully to the portfolio's growth.

For this reason, individual equity holdings should never make up less than 5% of a portfolio. In turn, regular rebalancing of assets to equal dollar weights is essential for achieving the higher long-term results that this innovative and proven approach may produce.

By definition, investing is never risk-free - recession, inflation, global catastrophes, unrelenting worldwide competition, evolving technology, increasing taxes, corporate failure, profit shortfalls, etc.

Despite this, risks of this nature can be minimized to acceptable levels through preceding study, prudent asset allocation, and proper diversification - those golden principles again!

Controlling or hedging against risk can also be accomplished by using sophisticated derivatives whose value is "derived" from changes in forces affecting stock and bond prices.

For instance, a grain farmer may sell a contract to lock in the price of his crop, while a customer, such as a food processor, may purchase a derivative from the grain farmer to lock in the price of raw materials.

In the end, derivatives can be used to insure portfolios against capital and income loss, hence being highly effective at leveraging, i.e., boosting investment returns through borrowing. However, they can be dangerous if excessive amounts are borrowed or utilized irresponsibly.

CHERRIES ON THE TOP.

Balance portfolios appropriately, diversify, and invest in a disciplined, systematic manner. In time there may be a sufficient cushion for higher-risk investment or even speculating for a one-time gain to augment the potential for wealth accumulation:

But always remember to investigate beforehand and only take such moves when portfolios have been built up properly, and the possible losses of greater risk-reward propositions can be afforded.

A last consideration is that effective investing, a long-term risk-reward proposition, must entail the ascent of never-ending walls of anxiety in a process involving many interdependent variables.

However, if you adhere to the two golden rules, exercise patience and self-discipline, you can be confident that your worry-free retirement will become a reality through outstanding and effective investing.

Remember, too, that time spent in the market will be far more essential than day-to-day timing while overcoming these walls of anxiety. The legendary Sir John Templeton once argued that the ideal investment moment was when one already had capital. Similarly, the great Warren Buffett has always viewed uncertainty and the discount chances it presents as a friend of the long-term investment value buyer.

Despite the complexities of modern investing, our parents never had such a vast selection of investment products and services from which to choose or on which to build their long-term retirement plans. Investing and prospering while effectively navigating the risk-reward balance is a challenge within our reach as never before.

For investors in today's enviable, fiscally-sound and enticingly "investable" secure haven for investment, comparable to none other!

CONCLUSION.

There is no doubt that wealth and prosperity are essential for happiness. Money may not give you other years of life, good health, or happiness, but it plays a vital function in society and is a powerful force that drives the global economy.

There is a Law of Wealth and Success in spirituality studies, and anyone who knows and applies these seven wealth production rules will prosper. Few people know these six principles since they are hidden from our eyes, which see only tangible objects and are beyond common comprehension.

Ancient sages from many civilizations and religions were familiar with the SIX laws of creating riches. They are universal; therefore, anyone of any faith can use them to achieve extraordinary achievement.

It is also essential to regard money as a source of divine energy. Everyone is mindful of it, but you must make it manifest. It is only necessary to externalize it. In other words, until you cultivate a "millionaire mentality," it is hard to attract wealth into your life.

Do not dislike money. If this energy is appropriately channeled and combined with the creative harmony of the universe, your positive, powerful thoughts can manifest everything you desire in your life.

Doesn't everyone like the money? People may subconsciously reject money based on religious principles, although receiving it overtly. You must love money as completely and devotedly as you love your partner.

Love money without arrogance, and it will return the favor. Do not consider it to be wicked or question its nature. Money is not unclean; only the brains of those who possess it are. You condemn, you lose.

Financial security is achieved through a procedure. It implies that this process will accompany you throughout your life, and by opening your heart and mind to riches, you will develop a sense of wealth that no one can take away.

Ideas are energy impulses that can materialize; consequently, one must realize that his or her life's destiny is contained entirely within his or her thoughts. Therefore, become accustomed to thinking about ease, riches, and success; the best will come to you. Do not loathe yourself!

When money enters your life, it is subservient to a goal, a goal, or a desire. Life's driving force has a purpose; it gives existence meaning and makes it sacred. It is up to you to determine your life's purpose.

You must explicitly identify how you want riches to manifest in your life, as it has multiple manifestations. From now on, establish your life goal as possible and adhere to it until it is accomplished.

Money is an energy, and all energies must circulate; therefore, money must be circulated in the same manner as blood. When blood flows easily throughout your body, your health is superb. Therefore, keep your money moving. This does not preclude saving. You must save it based on the emotion of life optimism.

People believe that holding savings protects them against "rainy days," yet this belief is based on pessimism, which is not promoted regarding money circulation. Do not constantly be afraid.

Therefore, saving money, so long as it is motivated by healthy, pleasant attitudes, will not impede the passage of money or cosmic energy in the cosmos.

Acquiring wealth without giving back generates negative karma, which will eventually manifest. The universe will reward you more if you are generous, selfless, truthful, and modest without being arrogant or hypocritical.

Giving and receiving extend beyond the realm of material goods. It may involve regard, flattery, or admiration for others. Therefore, expand your heart to give and accept more. Remember to express gratitude and appreciation to the Universe for the gift and be glad for what you currently possess.

Everyone has a "little voice" that speaks up when uncertain. The problem is that we have entirely blocked out the "small voice" The voice is truly your best friend in life and resides on the right side of your brain.

To consult your friend, construct a wish or inquiry in your heart and, preferably during meditation, allow whatever comes to flow. Therefore, whenever you meet an uncertain scenario, use your intuition for inspiration and guidance. Therefore, use your instincts in your moneymaking endeavors!

These are the six most effective money-making rules. They are the uncontested techniques to make riches in your life, so you should always have faith in them, as they have been tried and tested again throughout history. Implement them immediately, and your efforts will be well rewarded.

Do consult your spiritual direction if you are not sure. Apply them daily with self-assurance and perseverance, and you will soon start to notice miraculous results.

Management Skills for Managers.

- Time Management for Managers
- Employee Coaching for Managers
- Team Building for Managers
- Self Confidence for Managers
- Negotiation Skills for Managers
- Customer Service Skills for Managers
- Assertiveness for Managers
- Business Etiquette for Managers
- Listening Skills for Managers
- Leadership Skills for Managers
- Communication Skills for Managers
- Presentation Skills for Managers
- Stress Management for Managers
- Decision Making for Managers
- Conflict Management for Managers.

Series: Financial Freedom at Any Age.

- Achieving Financial Freedom in your 20's
- Achieving Financial Freedom in your 30's
- Achieving Financial Freedom in your 40's
- Achieving Financial Freedom in your 50's
- Achieving Financial Freedom in your 60's
- Achieving Financial Freedom in your 70's and beyond.
- Achieving Financial Freedom in children
- Achieving Financial Freedom in teenagers
- Achieving Financial Freedom in college students.
- Financial Scams to be Aware of in Retirement.

Series: Personal Finance for You.
- Buying and Selling Crypto for Beginners
- Why Investing in Dividend Stocks Makes Sense.

Series: Wealth 2022.

- Online Entrepreneurship.
- Starting Your Own Business
- Wealth Management
- Passive Income.
- 12 Steps to Starting your own business.

Series: Excellent Customer Service.

- Excellent Customer Service in Retail
- Excellent Customer Service in Fast Food
- Excellent Customer Service in Full-Service Restaurant
- Excellent Customer Service in Teaching.
- Excellent Customer Service in Real Estate
- Excellent Customer Service in a Call Center
- Excellent Customer Service as a Receptionist
- Excellent Customer Service in a Hotel
- Excellent Customer Service in Selling
- Excellent Customer Service No Matter the Situation.

- Excellent Customer Service in Dental Office
- Excellent Customer Service in Medical Office.

Series: Quick Money.

- Quick Money in a Week
- Quick Money in a Weekend
- Quick Money in a Month
- Quick Money for Students.

Series: How to Promote.

- How to Promote your Recipe Book
- How to Promote your Children's Book.

Other books by D.K. Hawkins.

- How to Make Your Business Thrive During a Recession
- Creating Surplus Value for Customers
- Recognizing Opportunities to Increase Cash Flow.
- Recessions are When Millionaires and Billionaires are Created.
- The Six Laws of Wealth

Author Bio

D.K. Hawkins. D.K. enjoys reading personal business books as well as spending time outdoors. More books will come in this collection, so please follow on Amazon for more books.

Thank you for your purchase of this book.

I honestly do appreciate it and appreciate you, my excellent customer.

God Bless You.

D.K. Hawkins.

www.ingramcontent.com/pod-product-compliance
Lightning Source LLC
Chambersburg PA
CBHW052351220526
45465CB00003BA/1055